The Reason

HELP AND HOPE
FOR
THOSE WHO GRIEVE

SALLY GRABLICK

4EVR PRESS · MICHIGAN

TO MY FAMILY

Joe, Katie, Ryan (and Maxx)

❧

You gave me a reason
to live, love and learn.
Thank you for believing in me,
and my ability to tell our story.

For Nancy
In Memory of your father
Believe!
Sally Grablick

CONTENTS

Contents

ACKNOWLEDGMENTS

Special recognition and sincere gratitude go to Teri Appel, Michael Leffler, and Danielle Dorman for reviewing, editing, and creating the necessary documents to prepare this manuscript for the publishing process. Your professionalism, kindness and support helped to make this book a reality.

With great respect and appreciation, I would like to thank the band Diamond Rio, The Compassionate Friends.org, Hay House, Inc. representing Doreen Virtue, PH.D., and Lynnette Brown, and author/ playwright Penn Kemp for granting me permission to use their photographs, website content, and quotes from published works in my book. The contribution of these items helps to enrich the content of my story and overall experience for my readers.

More thanks to: Lori Kesten, Bev Thomas, Nick Banaszak, Barrie and Judie Barber, David and Kim Hickmott, Shauna Shipman, my parents Jim and Nancy Hickmott, Elaine Mugan, Stephanie Atchison, Ant Kat, Kathy Ruggles, Chris Vacketta, and Becky Cubr, for your love, friendship, contributions (emails, photos, readings, technical assistance, shared experiences) and stanch support. You are my Earth Angels.

I would be remiss, if I did not recognize my husband Joe, and my daughter Katie, for the immeasurable amount of love, patience and support they have showered on me — during the writing of this book, and throughout our grieving process. I love you ...4EVR.

PREFACE

At 19 years of age, my son Ryan committed suicide — in our home, in his room, with a rifle. That is all I'm going to say about that. This isn't a story about how or why he took his life. It's a story of how his spirit returned to save mine.

In my desperation to endure this incomprehensible tragedy, I tried everything I could think of to release myself from the "black hole" of grief. But no drug, therapist, or book, was solely capable of giving me the peace or direction that Ryan ultimately did.

Before I go any further, let me make something perfectly clear. I do not claim to be an expert on anything beyond my own personal experience. I am not psychic, nor do I possess any extraordinary skills. I'm a mother who lost her son and wanted to know: "*Where did he go, and is he alright?*" It's that simple. I knew the mission, but didn't have a clue as to where it would lead me. This is the story of my journey...

INTRODUCTION

I went from walking five miles, five days a week, to sitting on my deck smoking a pack of cigarettes a day. Losing my son Ryan paralyzed me, both physically and emotionally. During the transition of life with him to life without him, I found it was easiest just to stay immobilized and concentrate on my breathing. In the earliest days of my grief it was really all I was capable of doing. If it had been easy to shut off my mind, I would have done that too.

My mind however had a life of its own, and it was running at warp speed. All the "could haves, should haves, and would haves" were spinning in my brain like a revolving door. Nothing I did had the ability to shut it down, believe me — I tried. In retrospect, I suppose that was a good thing, because it was the only part of me that seemed to be working, and it reminded me that I was still alive.

That was painful, because I didn't want to be alive. I didn't want to be in a world where Ryan wasn't. My whirling mind went into overdrive as I attempted to figure out a way to live without my son; but in my current state, I lacked the tools and direction required to accomplish this ominous task. A week after the suicide, my fate was drastically altered by a random encounter at a local department store...

I was forced to leave the deck that fateful day to shop for a container for Ryan's ashes. Back then, every single step was an obstacle to overcome — so making a trip to the store seemed like climbing Mt. Everest. I enlisted the assistance of my loving daughter, Katie, to get the job done.

Time spent with Katie forced me into "Mommy mode" and somehow it gave me the energy to get a few things done.

I ran into an old acquaintance while we were browsing the aisles of TJ Maxx. I hadn't seen this woman in several years and it surprised me that I recognized her at all. In fact, I had to re-introduce myself to her. We exchanged the usual "how are you" pleasantries and then I just blurted out "We're here to pick out a chest to put my son's ashes in."

That type of comment would scare the hell out of most people, but Margo just embraced me warmly and said, "I have lost both of my sons. You need to read *Life after Life* by Raymond Moody." I don't believe in coincidence; I believe everything happens for a reason. I wrote the title of the book down, selected the chest for Ryan's ashes, and headed straight for the book store.

I purchased that book and read it in two days. It opened up a new world of possibilities to me, and provided something I felt I could grab onto. Books became my salvation; before I knew it, I had become a Borders 'junkie'. There I could cruise the aisles and focus my attention on getting better, rather than constantly wallowing in my grief.

I found books that opened my mind and heart to things I'd never imagined could truly exist. Through them, I grew to find understanding in a world, that once familiar, had become so foreign to me. I discovered my spiritual side and began creating a whole new life for myself. It was what I needed to do. My life was forever changed, so I had to change with it. This book is to give hope to those who are browsing those same aisles right now — looking for answers. I hope my story will help you find some.

PART ONE

IN THE BEGINNING

It's Called Grief

I GUESS YOU COULD call me a "seeker." I've never been the type of person to accept something without trying to understand it first. I didn't understand death. My son Ryan's suicide shattered the ability to comprehend anything. I had been caught unaware and unprepared for the chaos his death created in our lives. It left me fumbling in a world I no longer recognized, numb with pain and struggling to survive. In the wake of his funeral, this state of confusion held me captive, and left me wondering, "Now what?"

Up to this point, I had followed the steps that were clearly outlined for me: sign the death certificate, select a funeral home, decide on the type of burial, pick out the coffin, chose an outfit for him, set the funeral arrangements, order flowers, etc. People walked me through these tasks because they had to be done. But, after the funeral, I found myself sitting at home in a space filled with condolence floral arrangements and plants wondering, "What the hell do I do now?" Nobody tells you that. There is no direction for the days following the funeral formalities, except "give it time."

How much time? That's what I wanted to know. I needed someone to tell me how long I was going to feel like someone had ripped my guts out and ran over the rest of me with a Mack truck. So I asked. I had to ask several people before I got my answer. It came from a family friend who had lost her son some 20 years before. She told me it took her five years. Her response was, "It took five years before I could open my eyes in the morning and not feel that heavy weight on my chest."

I was grateful to hear that for two reasons. First, now I could focus on being "better" in five years and this gave me a goal. Secondly, every day since it had happened, I had experienced that same feeling upon awakening. I would open my eyes, and think — my son is dead — which was followed by that same crushing weight she'd mentioned. It was paralyzing. Hearing her describe this had made me feel "normal".

I looked and saw that she was there, standing in front of me — alive. I needed to know that Ryan's death was something I could actually live through. I found myself looking at her from a completely different perspective. She wasn't just Betty; she was a SURVIVOR. A mother who had lost her child and had successfully found a way to live her life again. I made up my mind then and there to be a survivor too. I just needed the map out of hell to accomplish this.

I felt sick all over, so I started with my doctor. He prescribed antidepressants, which I took religiously, praying for some kind of relief. They didn't touch the pain, but they did keep me going. I also was having a lot of trouble sleeping, so he gave me something for that too. I knew that these would not cure my grief, but I felt like I was at least making an effort to do something. No one I knew was really offering me any advice on what I should do. Even now, I marvel at the thought that there was no direction — no "to do's" for the grieving process that anyone seemed able to guide me to.

I stuck with the doctor theme and started seeing a counselor. I picked someone who was familiar with my family and our situation, hoping it would help. It was a godsend. There, I was free to talk about Ryan and this brought me great comfort. I couldn't do that anywhere else, or so it seemed. There was too much pain in my house to discuss him there. My parents and other family members were all working through their anguish too. We all seemed to be dealing with the pain alone, in little silos, away from each other. At my grief counseling sessions it was comforting to have another live body in the room as I wept and recalled memories of my son. I went there looking for a lifeline to grab onto, one that would lead me out of the maze of my pain.

My counselor was able to suggest the use of what was referred to as "EMDR" (Eye Movement Desensitization and Reprocessing). It is often used to treat post-traumatic stress. It has proven to be an effective way to decrease/eliminate the symptoms people exhibit after witnessing tragic events. Suicide qualified as a tragic event. It helped me. I was also able to convince my husband Joe, my daughter Katie and my father to use EMDR too. They needed it more than I did.

Joe and Katie had found Ryan after the suicide, so they were working with a different deck of cards than I was. My father, who lives right down the road from us, had been called after the discovery of Ryan's body. He had rushed down to our house and been exposed to the same horrific sight as Joe and Katie. That was why they all needed EMDR more than me. I had been at work that morning and therefore was spared that scene. I have always felt that Ryan made a conscious choice to do it after I'd already left for the day. Somewhere inside the fog of his pain — he had thought of me, and I loved him more because of it.

So, in the earliest days following the suicide, the counseling sessions became a part of our routine. Outside of that, our schedules had little in common. My husband Joe spent most of his time away from the house. If he wasn't working, he was at the golf course. My daughter Katie went into perpetual motion. She worked all the hours she could get and then would make plans with her friends after work. When she chose to spend time at home, she spent it sleeping or working on jigsaw puzzles. I couldn't seem to leave the house, except for the counseling appointments or to replenish my cigarette supply. It wasn't much, but at least we were all still breathing.

Being home for me was a double-edged sword. I was afraid to leave, but also afraid to be there alone, not so much during the day — but at night. This was something new to me. I had never been scared in my own home. Katie exhibited fear as well. She could not go downstairs to her bedroom alone. Because of this, we moved her things upstairs and turned my office into a temporary bedroom for her. I had my husband put a door stop on the basement door, and insisted this door stay open any time I was down there. The very thought of being shut downstairs made me hysterical. All of this was due to the fact that Ryan's room was also downstairs, and we didn't want to be alone where he had chosen to end his life.

Our laundry room is on the lower level too. This made the one thing I felt capable of doing an exercise in endurance. When I found myself home alone, I would stand at the top of the stairs and say out loud, "Ryan, I have to go downstairs now, so don't decide to show up while I'm alone or it will scare the bageeberz out of me." Ryan had been an obedient child, so giving him direction seemed like the right thing to do. Somewhere inside of me, I believed he could hear me, and saying this made it easier to descend the stairs.

Other equally bizarre behavior evolved from the suicide. I found myself moving from room to room at dusk, flipping on every light in the house. I kept most of the televisions on, regardless of day or night, to keep from feeling alone. The patio doors facing the pool suddenly required window blinds after being bare for several years. At nightfall, I would lower the new blinds and shut them tightly. We ordered French doors with blinds and had them installed to enclose the foyer, further isolating the entrance to the lower level.

It wasn't any specific thing we were afraid of in the house; we were just experiencing backlash from the shocking experience we had all just been through. A catastrophic event had taken place in our "comfort zone", and these strange behaviors were our way of coping. When we couldn't cope, we simply avoided the location of the tragedy. By "not seeing," we did not have to "believe" it had actually taken place. Sadly, these were only temporary solutions to a now permanent situation.

All of this made me realize that we were going to need more help if we were going to recover. I took my usual course of action and turned to reading to gather the information I felt we would need to accomplish this task. I didn't have to worry about what books to read, because the books found me. This was a blessing in disguise because I wasn't capable of making many decisions at this stage of the game. Even little choices tended to overwhelm me.

My friends were excellent resources when it came to reading material. Some books were given to me, others were mentioned within the text of the current books I was reading, or they would simply be recommended to me in conversation. I kept a running list and had plenty of titles to select from when I needed a new book. Reading made me feel better. It made me feel like I was doing something. I gathered valuable information from the books and the time I spent reading at home helped me to become more comfortable there.

This was not the case for my husband and daughter. They were very uncomfortable in the house, and simply didn't like to be there. I understood that. It was a no-brainer. Katie was only 17 when Ryan died. The trauma of the event itself would kill most people in their tracks, but Katie stayed strong. I said to her the day before the funeral, "Baby, its okay to cry." She just looked at me and said, "No, Mom. Ryan is making me strong for you, and when you're better I'll take my turn." I was coping with it in my way and so I had to extend the same courtesy to her. All I could do was keep a watchful eye on my daughter, and pray that she would be okay.

My husband would never say he was afraid. Joe could go up and down the stairs without any fuss, but he did not go into Ryan's bedroom. For the most part, he could easily avoid being in the house most of the time without it seeming to be intentional. After all, it was summer and he had to take care of the lawn and pool. He spent a lot of time at the golf course with his friends, or tinkering in the garage. It was a somewhat normal routine for him so it did not seem like avoidance.

Joe, like Katie, appeared to be so strong. I remember thinking, "How can they be doing so well after what they had seen and been through? Why was I the one struggling so hard?" The answer was shock. We all seemed to be somewhat normal; however, in actuality, we were walking time bombs. Unknowingly, the true impact of our grief was there waiting, just below the surface.

All of this, and more, made the case for *not* selling the house. I think this surprised a lot of people. We did list the house, only to pull the listing a week or so later due to my gut instincts. It just did not feel like the right thing to do. We needed to face the truth of what had happened. We could run, but we would never be able to hide from the reality that Ryan was gone — forever. Conquering our fears in the same atmosphere that housed them would be one of our biggest challenges, but I felt it had to be done. I approached it as a conditioning exercise, thinking that the more time we spent there the easier it would get, and it did — eventually.

I saw our recovery in two phases. First, we were going to have to address the suicide itself and learn to cope with the horror of this violent act. Then, we needed to work through the grief of our loss, and the fact that Ryan had made a choice we were all going to have to live with.

I did not want us to remain the huge gaping sores we'd become — walking around without a scab for the rest of our lives. I was determined to find a way for us to heal. I became a "Grief Pioneer," and was soon blazing unfamiliar trails for my family, looking for help, *looking for hope.*

2

BITS AND PIECES

I struggled to get some sleep the evening after the suicide. It was our first night without Ryan. I was so tired, but sleep eluded me. Finally, just before dawn, I dropped into the abyss. I had a dream that I was standing in a large space filled with white fog. Out of nowhere came my son's voice. He said, "Mom, we can talk just like this. You don't even have to move your lips." I could hear him so clearly! Then boom — I snapped out of my deep sleep, as if I'd been dropped from the sky. My eyes flew open. His words repeated in my mind, over, and over again.

What was that? It felt too real to be a dream and yet there I was, still in bed. I didn't quite know what to make of it, except I knew that it was important enough to remember, so I wrote it down. Telepathic, that's what Ryan was trying to tell me. Communication without speaking — was this possible? I was in too much pain to wrap my mind around it, but his words would not let me go.

That morning we went to the funeral home to make arrangements. At this point, I was obsessed with seeing my son. I had not been allowed to see him at home after the suicide. I was told that I could see him at the hospital where they took his body to draft the death certificate, but my request to see him there was denied as well. So, the first thing I asked of the funeral director was to see my son. He did not want me to do this and cautiously tried to explain why, in efforts to discourage my request. I knew that seeing Ryan's face would be impossible due to the circumstances of the suicide, but I did not relent. Instead, I found a way to compromise. I asked if he could cover Ryan up, and just pull out his hand for me so I could touch him and have the chance to say goodbye. The director looked at me with kindness and compassion, and agreed that this much could be done.

I was terrified. I can hardly tell you how completely paralyzed with fear I was at that moment — I don't know why. All I know is that I clenched the cross hanging from my necklace, repeating over, and over again, "Face your fear...Face your fear…" as I slowly descended the stairs of the funeral home, to the basement where Ryan's body was.

My husband, daughter and I entered the room where he lay on a gurney draped in sheets. Joe and I stood on one side of him, and Katie stood on the other. In the silence, I reached for Ryan's hand. *It was so cold.* I noticed that he had a small cut on his finger and all I could think about was how I wanted to put a band-aid on it. I leaned over, kissed his finger, and then cupped my hand over his. I whispered to him softly and told him many times over that circumstances were not so bad that it warranted taking his life. Then, I told him ever so clearly, "Ryan, I need to talk to you. I need answers. You know what I am going to do. I am going to see Elaine — please be there." Truthfully, I do not know where those words came from, but I spoke them.

I pulled myself up and stood erect with my hand still cupping Ryan's. I looked at my daughter and then my husband. Slowly Joe reached out and covered my hand with his own. Katie followed suit, putting her hand over Joe's. We stood there, united in silence — our last time as a family of four. We all felt the significance of that moment, and the weight of it was *unbearable.*

I don't know how long we stood there. I do not remember letting go. I only remember staring at the sheet that covered my child's face. I wanted to kiss him so badly, but knew that this could never be. If Joe and Katie had not been there with me I would have done it, but as it was, I could not. Reality hit me like a tidal wave and I realized for the first time the meaning of the word FOREVER. It was crushing, immobilizing, and terrifying to feel like this. I could sense that the life was slowly draining out of me. I felt so completely helpless, realizing I could do nothing to change what had happened. My only recourse was to find a way to live with it, except right then — I did not feel that living with it was even a remote possibility.

When we got into our car to leave, Katie asked me if I had noticed the cut on Ryan's finger; I acknowledged that I had. "I wanted to put a band-aid on it," she told me. I looked at my daughter's face trying to imagine the horror of what she'd experienced these past few days. In her eyes, I saw the pain and anguish her face had managed to disguise. "Me too," was all I could say.

There was so much to deal with; I felt completely overwhelmed. Like Scarlett O'Hara, my mind kept repeating, "I can't think about it now…I'll think of it tomorrow…" I turned to my husband and asked him to drive to the florist next. All I could do was *what I had to do* at that moment in time. I had to remind myself to inhale, exhale, and just put one foot in front of the other. These were all the tools I had and so I used them. We went from one task to the next doing things we never imagined we'd have to do, but we did them, and we did them together as a family.

When it comes to my memory, the early days of grief kind of run together. I can't always tell you the exact day a certain thing happened, but I can recall with certainty specific events that took place. Somewhere between picking out the flowers for the casket and the day of the funeral service, I banked a few of those said events in my mind. I kept them there for later review, hoping to understand them better when I came out of the ether.

One event took place as I sat in the living room late one evening watching television. My husband was on the floor dozing and my

daughter was asleep in our room. I was channel surfing and I paused to watch an old movie. I had been watching it for less than five minutes when the man on the screen spoke this line several times: "I gotta get a woman, I gotta get a woman." It snapped me into total awareness because when Ryan was about 13, he started saying that all the time. I'm sure we heard that said a million times between the ages of 13 and 15. It had driven us *insane*. I remembered asking him once where he'd picked up that crazy phrase. He just smiled at me and said, "Some old movie."

I had just talked about "I gotta get a woman" that very day with my brother, David. He was writing Ryan's eulogy and we had spent the better part of that morning reminiscing about all the special things that were my son. I could not stop thinking how very odd it was that out of nowhere, and after all this time, the movie he had spoken of was playing right in front of me. It made the hair on the back of my neck stand straight up. Could this be Ryan making an attempt to get my attention? If it was, *it worked.*

Another evening one of Ryan's buddies, Gabe, came over and we sat on the deck sharing stories about him. Gabe asked if I remembered the time I had asked them to transplant some bushes. I confirmed that I did. He smiled, and then told me that when I'd gone back into the house, Ryan had beaten on the bushes with the shovel a couple of times and said "These stupid things won't grow here, it's all clay!" They had joked and laughed their way through the chore with Ryan whacking away at those poor bushes the entire time. We had a good chuckle as we gazed out at the bushes now growing by the pool. Of the four originally planted, three had survived and were thriving.

We both looked up when Katie suddenly darted out of the house. Visibly shaken, she stood before us and said, "Wow, I just had the weirdest thing happen! A song was playing in my head, and when I put on my earphones that same song was playing — and it was on exactly the same verse that I was."

A day or so later, Katie had another peculiar incident occur. She had spent the entire evening working on a puzzle in the living room, but couldn't finish it because one piece was missing. We all helped her look. We searched under the sofa, the seat cushions, and on the floor surrounding the table — but found nothing. Exhausted from the day, we all decided to go to bed thinking we'd find it in the morning.

When I woke up, I walked into the living room and saw that a single puzzle piece was laying in full view on the corner of the table. It was adjacent to the puzzle itself, which lay waiting to be completed. I asked my husband if he had found it. He said no. When Katie got up, I pointed to the puzzle piece, and clarified that neither Joe nor I had found it. Apparently, it had simply "appeared" while we were all sleeping. Silently she picked up the missing piece and placed it into the puzzle. "Thanks Ryan" she said softly. We all stood there — spellbound.

A few days after the funeral, several of our household appliances began giving me trouble. It started with the microwave. I would attempt to reheat something and it would just stop in the middle of the cycle. I'd open the door, close it, hit restart, but nothing would happen. Then, all of the sudden it would come back on. A repair man came out and put a small piece in it, but the next day it started acting up again. The power issue persisted for several days. Exasperated, I said out loud, "Ryan stop messing with the microwave. Service calls cost money!" The microwave issues stopped immediately, but that's when our television decided to take on a life of its own. I would walk into a room and all the sudden the TV would turn on. The second or third time this happened to me, I sat down and just stared at the TV in wonder. What in the world was going on?

I took some time and wrote a list of all the "crazy" things that were

happening. It kept coming back to the same question — Was this Ryan? Elaine popped into my head again. I needed to see if I could locate her. Maybe she could help me. Why not? At this point, I had nothing to lose.

3

Talking to Ryan

THE FIRST TIME I met Elaine I happened to be going through my divorce from Ryan and Katie's father. I had asked several people if they knew a psychic I could see. It was a very uncertain time in my life and I thought that a little peek into the future might benefit me. One day a co-worker provided me with Elaine's name and number, so I gave her a call.

I found her to be quite gifted and in the years that followed I would see her occasionally just for fun. I didn't take it in a completely serious way. For me, it was more of a vague view of what might come to pass. I started out being very skeptical. I tend to be the type of person that needs to have something "real" to substantiate things. I believe that most of us are programmed this way. We are taught to disbelieve what we cannot physically see, touch or hear. In that respect I was no different, except I was curious about the possibilities, and I could feel myself opening up a little more each time I visited her.

I had never asked Elaine to communicate with the dead. I didn't even know if it was something she could do. All I knew was that I needed some help and she was the only person I could think of to ask for assistance. I could not ignore that little voice inside my head that kept pulling me in Elaine's direction. One major change I made immediately after Ryan's death was to pay attention to my instincts. I had vowed after that day to never ignore them again, and I haven't. So, I followed my intuition and put what little energy I had into tracking her down.

Elaine's old phone number was no longer in service, but thank God for the internet. I located the proper website used to retrieve phone numbers, and when I typed in her name, it handed her right to me. While I was on a roll, I decided to pick up the telephone and gave her a call. As luck would have it, she answered the phone and we were able to book an appointment for the following afternoon.

I called a friend of mine and asked if she would accompany me. I needed her to write notes for me during the reading. The skeptic lurking inside of me also felt that it would be a good idea to take someone else along as another set of eyes and ears, in the event that my need to connect with Ryan threatened to override my common sense.

I was anxious to see Elaine, and decided to prepare for our appointment by packing a little bag containing a few of Ryan's personal belongings. I offered her the bag when I arrived at her home the next day for my reading, but she declined it. She didn't want me to show or tell her anything about the subject of my concerns. She was adamant about preserving the authenticity of the information she would be delivering to me during the reading.

This was the second time Elaine had stated the need for confidentiality. When I had called to set up the appointment, I had told her my name and that I had lost my son. She had interrupted me immediately, asking me not to share any further details. I honored her request and we simply set up the time for the reading. It was her insistence on privacy that established the foundation of trust between us. This created a more relaxed atmosphere, allowing me to remain open to the information I was about to receive.

Elaine sat on the opposite side of the room rubbing her hands together, looking into the rug that lay on the floor between us. After a moment or two, she looked up at me shaking her head. "Oh dear" she said, "Ryan, what have you done?" She told me my son had taken his own life and then she proceeded to give details about things only Ryan could possibly know.

Elaine began by talking about Ryan's depression. He told her that he had struggled with it for the past 7 years; it started when he was about 12. This helped me to better understand our current situation, but did little to ease the guilt I felt rising inside of me. Perhaps he sensed this, because he made it a point to say, "Don't worry Mom, I'm okay. It's not your fault."

Ryan expressed that he was ashamed of the way he left, but he also made it very clear that he had wanted to make a statement, and because of that, would do it again. As it stood, he had no regrets. When I started to cry, he attempted to joke, because he could never bear to see me in tears. He said, "Remember the bushes Mom; remember the pantry."

I have already told the story of the bushes that he and Gabe planted, but let me explain the pantry. This was something special Ryan and I shared to fool Katie. She made a fuss every time I bought sweets, because she couldn't resist them. So, when I bought goodies I'd tell Ryan my secret hiding place in the pantry. This way he could get some treats when he wanted them and Katie was none the wiser.

Ryan spoke lovingly of his sister and asked me to tell her to study hard. He said that he felt bad he hadn't been more focused on Katie, but reassured me that he would be watching over her. Ryan also stated that he was using music to communicate with her, which explained the earlier incident she'd had with the earphones.

Elaine said that Ryan wanted to tell my husband Joe "hello" and that he loved him. He successfully validated this message by showing her a large pair of hands and a table saw. Those things illustrated an accident my husband had one day while working with Ryan on our house; Joe had nearly cut his thumb off using the circular saw. Only a family member would know these details.

He also brought up my brother David and said, "Thanks — that was really nice." Ryan had a special way of saying "really nice"; it was a standard expression of his. She said Ryan smiled and laughed when he

said it, as if he didn't deserve all the nice things David had said about him in the eulogy — but he did appreciate it.

Then Ryan threw a curve ball. He started to insist that we cover his grandpa up with "the blanket." Tilting her head to the side, Elaine asked me if there was a special blanket Ryan and his grandfather had shared. Over, and over again, he kept showing it to her, claiming it would make his grandpa feel better if we let him have it. I knew of no such blanket. I had no idea what Ryan was talking about, but I made sure this was written down so I could ask my dad about it later.

Ryan brought up his favorite green Ralph Lauren shirt and instructed me to keep it. He loved that shirt. I must have washed and ironed that thing a million times. Oddly enough, the day before the suicide, I'd found it on the floor of his closet and had simply re-hung it since I was tired of reminding him to pick up his clothes. It was a blessing to have had done that—because after the fact, I was able to bury my nose in the shirt and inhale the scent of him that still lingered there. I had in fact been spending a lot of time with that shirt since he'd passed. I guess he must have seen me. Elaine stated that Ryan's eyes were filled with "big crocodile tears" and he was promising me that I would get the big hug I'd been asking for in my sleep, in my dreams.

She paused for a moment and then continued. Smiling, Elaine said, "He's eating a big, heaping bowl of spaghetti — do you know why?" This made me laugh! Growing up, Ryan had gone through a "Godfather" period. He loved the movies and watched them by series. Other series favorites were Indiana Jones, Die Hard, John Wayne, Monty Python, and James Bond.

He'd been stuck on the "Godfather" films for awhile. During this period, I had earned the nickname "Momma Mia", and spent a lot of time cooking him pasta and listening to him profess how he wished he'd been born Italian. Eventually this phase passed, but my nickname stuck.

From that day forward, I was "Momma Mia" or "Momma" for short. It was a quirky little thing we'd shared and remembering it made me miss him even more.

The reading was winding down. That's when he brought up "the letter." Ryan had left us a suicide letter on his computer screen. The way the letter was written made it sound as if he were speaking to me, but the fact is, he did not address it to any one of us in particular. I believe that the letter was written to absolve us all from guilt; he made me feel that was his intention. In truth, there is nothing anyone can say in a suicide note to remove the burden of guilt. Everyone feels responsibility when it is suicide. Therefore, it did not bring the closure I believe he wanted it to.

Elaine asked me then if I had any questions. I was not prepared for that. I had come here with nothing but questions; however, I was so bowled over by the content of the reading I could not think of one. I told her to tell him that I loved him. "He knows that," she said with certainty, "and he loves you too."

I sat in silence. The reading had far exceeded my expectations. Nothing he'd relayed had been extraordinarily profound. What Ryan had given me were many small, personal facts. He had been careful to talk about things that were ours and ours alone. These specific details helped to confirm that Ryan had indeed been present at the reading.

It was in embracing this truth that I felt a sense of peace. I closed my eyes and savored the moment. I had a feeling it would not last, but that was okay. Because in that space and time, I had felt my son's presence, and for the first time since the suicide, I felt hope. It was the reason I had come here, and you can be sure — I took it with me.

4

The Blanket

I reviewed the notes that were taken during the reading as we drove home from Elaine's. I even allowed cynicism to play itself out by reviewing each detail from a skeptics point of view, but found I could not refute the fact that Ryan was the only one capable of providing all of the personal details that had been given. I can describe in one word how it made me feel to come to this conclusion — INCREDIBLE.

I was completely wowed by the amount of information I'd received. The bulk of it had made complete sense during the reading itself; little was left unresolved. I knew from other readings that it was normal to have left over pieces of information. One of the pieces I was anxious to resolve regarded "the blanket" Ryan had mentioned. Later that evening I went to see my parents, hoping they could solve that mystery for me.

Mom and Dad like to sit in their garage on summer evenings and watch the cars go by. That's where I found them when I pulled into the driveway. I explained to them where I had been that afternoon. My mother is a believer in the afterlife, and was open to the discussion. As a rule, my dad is not the type of person who thinks or talks about those things. In fact, I would have described him as the world's biggest skeptic — but Ryan's death had changed everyone and I watched as my father listened intently to the details of my reading.

When I got to the part where Ryan told me to "cover Grandpa up with the blanket," I looked directly at my dad and asked if he and Ryan had a favorite blanket that they'd shared? He said "No" and then turned to look at my mother. This prompted her to tell me about the quilt she had sewn for his 20th birthday, which happened to be just a few days away. As she spoke, tears welled up in her eyes. She said, "I had a feeling I was supposed to give it to him early — but didn't. Now he'll never know that I made it for him." I felt certain that this quilt was the blanket he had referred to in the reading.

I suddenly realized that my son had given me the perfect item for validation. Neither Ryan nor I had any knowledge that this quilt even existed until *after* his death, so to have him acknowledge it in the reading confirmed his presence for me completely. I pointed this simple fact out to my mother. It became clear to all of us that Ryan was now aware of the special blanket his grandmother had made for him. I encouraged her to give it to my dad, because that is what Ryan had requested.

Looking at my parents, it was plain to see that our conversation have given them a little of what I had brought home with me that afternoon — hope. I did not see shock or disbelief, as I had feared I would. It was clear that the information provided during the reading had been capable of opening their hearts and minds as it had mine. This, and the fact that the reading was so well validated, gave me a euphoric lift. I decided to ride the wave of relief for as long as I could. It was my first real break out of the black hole and I wanted to enjoy it.

At Ryan's funeral, a friend of mine told me there would be little "hooks" I would find along the path of grief that would give me some relief from the pain. She had said, "Squeeze all you can out of them before you reach for the next one." I didn't quite understand what she had meant at the time, but I do now. Like an aerial acrobat, you swing from one glimmer of hope to the next (hook by hook) in order to make your way across the channel of grief. This reading was my first real hook, and I was hanging on *tight*.

5

Cliff Notes for the Beginner

It was about this time that I began to wonder — how is it we are taught to love, work, marry, and procreate, but no one teaches us how to grieve? I had experienced nothing at this point to prepare me for this cruel twist of fate. Clearly, I was going to need more direction than "give it time" if I was going to make it through this hell.

Back in the day, there was a Mourning Handbook. But somehow, through the generations, it was lost. The Victorians had it down to a science. They even had a parlor in their homes where they hosted the funerals of deceased family members. That's where the term funeral "parlor" came from. People wore black for a designated length of time, and grieving families were not asked to socialize. The only thing expected of them was to rest and recover from their loss. As chunks of time passed, certain "social privileges" were reinstated.

Those guidelines seemed worth resurrecting; I especially liked the rest and recover strategy. This was exactly the type of direction I was looking for. I couldn't help but think that a step-by-step guide for grieving in the 21st century existed somewhere. All I can say is that if one exists, it did not cross my path. Due to the lack of availability, I decided to create my own "Mourner's Guide." Even in my state of confusion, I realized that if the basic issues could be identified, they would be a whole lot easier to deal with. Due to the circumstances of Ryan's death, I included a few that relate specifically to suicide.

✓ **#1 Tell the Truth. (Suicide specific)**

Too often families will lie about the cause of an unnatural death, due to the shame/guilt that is often associated with them. We found that telling the truth about Ryan's suicide left little room for lies or innuendo. All that was left to question was the reason why our son had chosen to take his life, and that was something no one except Ryan would ever really know for sure.

✓ **#2 Control the ripple effect. (Suicide specific)**

Everybody and their brother will approach you and tell you that they feel guilty about something they could or should have said or done. This is something you can control by NOT speculating. Hug them, thank them for their concern, but always keep sight of the facts. Don't get caught up in their need for absolution. Your number one priority is you and your immediate family. Address the concerns within that nucleus, and stay focused on recovery.

✓ **#3 Take the help offered from family and friends.**

Fatigue besieged each waking hour. I didn't have the energy to clean my house or cook my family dinner. In pre-grief days, you could have eaten off my toilet seats. Now, our socks were sticking to the floors. Due to my lack of energy, I decided to take my friends up on their offers to help. All I had to do was make a simple phone call and they came running. They were actually grateful I had asked for help. My friend Cathy came over and scrubbed our house from top to bottom. Other friends and family prepared food for us, and when that ran out — there was takeout. Having someone to turn to got us over the first hump, and reminded us how lucky we were to have such wonderful and supportive people in our lives.

✓ **#4 Take time off to grieve.**

Two weeks after the funeral, the very thought of returning to the office still completely overwhelmed me. How could I return to work when I could barely make it out of bed? Not to mention the fact, that my powers of concentration had all but abandoned me. To put it bluntly, grief was sucking the life out of me and that didn't leave much to offer an employer. I ended up taking six months off from my job. I understand not everyone needs that length of time to get back on their feet, but I did. I believe it is important to take the time you need to get yourself together. You aren't going to be any good to anyone else until you do.

✓ **#5 It's okay to grieve at your own pace —
your own way.**

It is a fact that we all grieve differently. I expected my family to feel exactly the *way* I did, *when* I did. If they didn't, it hurt and confused me. My counselor helped me with this by pointing out a simple fact. All of our actions and reactions would be different, simply because we were. What was important is that we all understood that this was normal. It took the pressure off to know that although we were all grieving, we weren't all expected to approach it in the same way.

✓ **#6 People say STUPID things.**

Losing a child is the worst loss anyone can experience. So, unless you have lost a child — never say that you understand — because you don't. It doesn't compare to losing a parent, sibling or pet. It isn't like sending a daughter away for summer camp or a son to college for the first time. It isn't even close. "They're in a better place," or "You have to move on," are a few of the things people are taught to say to the bereaved — but shouldn't. When grief is fresh, it's hard to believe that *anyplace* is better than home and "moving on" is the last thing on your mind. I don't believe people say these things to intentionally hurt anyone — It's just that they don't know any better.

✓ **#7 The first year of mourning is one step forward, three steps back.**

It is a fact that the first year is the worst. Getting through all the "firsts" (first birthday, Christmas, Mother's Day, etc.) without them is a real challenge. I remember thinking, "I want to feel better now!" Unfortunately, it takes time and work to heal. That first year nearly *kicked my ass*, but I forced myself to work through the pain. For the most part, the death of a loved one isn't something you "get over." Grief is a process; we become much better at *coping* with loss as time marches forward.

✓ **#8 Don't make any major decisions/changes in the first year.**

A friend of mine pulled me aside at the funeral home and told me that I shouldn't worry about anything except maintaining the status quo for a least a year. As guidance goes, it was by far — the best I was given. Don't sell your home, get a divorce, or quit your job. Your emotions are on a roller coaster that first year, and it is not the time to make life-altering decisions. Everyday life will be enough of a challenge for you to get through. Just do the best you can, with what you have, until your life regains some form of stability again.

✓ **#9 Brace yourself — Grief triggers are everywhere.**
Grief has its own agenda. I never knew when or how it would strike. There are little things called "triggers" that grief uses to knock your legs out from underneath you. These triggers can be people, places, objects, or songs — literally anything that recalls a special memory of your loved one. For example, one day while in the grocery store I came upon a shelf of chili beans. Ryan loved my chili and seeing those cans of beans was all that it took. My breath started to come in small bursts and I closed my eyes tight in an effort to hold back the tears. I lost that battle, and soon found myself sobbing uncontrollably in aisle five. Those darn beans were a trigger. I told my mother, "I don't know what I am going to do if I can't even get through the supermarket without crying." There is no point in worrying about something like this because it is out of your control. You just have to deal with it when it hits, and work your way through it.

✓ **#10 Have a plan for the holidays and special occasions.**
Holidays, birthdays, anniversaries, and special events are

easier to get through if you have a plan. Don't wing it or you'll end up sitting home alone and feeling miserable. Schedule the entire day and fill it with things to do, places you can go, and people you can see. Change your regular routine and give these days a new feel. If you always cook Christmas dinner, then ask another family member to do it this time; maybe just plan to spend the holiday out of town. No matter what you do, you will still be thinking of them, but if you keep moving, you won't be dwelling on the pain. Think of a way to honor your loved one on these occasions by doing things like lighting a candle, reading a poem, or saying a special prayer for them. This will help the lingering sorrow because it is a way to acknowledge their memory, and nothing feels more important to us than to know that they are being remembered.

✓ **#11 When all else fails — just breathe.**

The day of the suicide, I called my friend Natalie. She had to listen to me cry on the telephone, because she lived hundreds of miles away in San Diego, California. I kept telling her over, and over, "I don't know if I can take this — What am I going to do?" Patiently, she listened as I purged my pain into the phone lines. When I finally fell silent, she said to me in soft, gentle tone "When you can't do anything else Sal, just breathe." I will never forget the simplicity of her words nor the comfort that they brought to me. She had resolved my immediate quandary with one little word — *breathe*. That much I could do...

I was in hell and needed to find a way out. Defining the mourning basics was a good start. My grief counselor once told me, "It says…I walk *through* the valley of the shadow of death…It doesn't say build a condo and *live there*." He helped me understand that the only way to deal with grief was to go through it. If you try to go around grief, you're just delaying the inevitable. My mission was clear, and I wasn't going to find the answers if I got stuck or tried to go around the mourning process. I made number twelve my mission statement:

✓ **#12 No Condo's in the valley and no giving up —
it's all about SURVIVAL.**

6

REPRIEVE

THE BLACK HOLE IS a place of darkness, filled with heartache and despair. In the beginning, I was powerless over its gravitational pull. Without warning, it would swallow me up and hold me captive. Inside this dark void my ability to think, move, or rationalize was stripped away — rendering me defenseless. It took time, but eventually I managed to find a few tools that enabled me to climb out at will. My problem was that I was spending more time *inside* of the black hole than I was *out*.

It took three weeks for the initial shock of Ryan's suicide to wear off. By then all ceremonial tasks had been completed. When the dust settled — *the real pain kicked in*. It was as if we'd had our backs to an advancing tidal wave, which finally hit the shore. It struck us hard. This pain was crushing and much more intense than the first few weeks of grief. It turned out that the initial blow of heartache had merely been an introduction to the real agony that had been waiting in the wings. All I could do was pray that our pain had finally reached its threshold, and hope that we would soon regain the foothold necessary to pull ourselves through.

Much of my own pain was created from the fact that I couldn't stop thinking about Ryan. He was on my mind night and day. I ached for the sight of him and found myself looking for him everywhere I went. I scanned passing cars, crowded sidewalks, and all the public places I frequented yearning to catch a glimpse of him. I foolishly hoped that he would magically appear and tell me that this had all just been some kind of cruel joke. At night, I would dream of this happening, only to awaken and find that he was still gone.

I found myself bargaining with God, saying I didn't care what it would take to bring him back to me. I was prepared to give everything I owned, including my own soul, to make it so. It was hard for me to accept that this was never going to be anything I could fix, buy or beg for. The hopelessness of the situation began taking its toll on me. As a result, my hook from the reading was wearing thin.

It hadn't been a complete drought; little "things" had continued to happen throughout the summer. The little signs we received helped to prolong the life of my hook, but I had a sinking feeling that they weren't going to be enough. Ryan must have felt that too because he persistently tried new ways to make contact with us.

One morning about a month or so after his death, Joe and I awoke to the smell of bacon frying. Our family ritual is that Joe makes a big breakfast for everyone on Sunday mornings. Ryan had told me several times, that he always knew what day of the week it was if he smelled bacon frying. Joe and I got up to investigate, thinking maybe Katie was planning to surprise us by cooking the family breakfast. But when we got to the kitchen, no one was there.

This was exciting! Something different…we talked about several possible causes, but ended up ruling them all out. The smell of bacon was strong in our bedroom and there was no reasonable explanation. As crazy as it sounded, we finally concluded that this was just Ryan — reminding us that it was Sunday, and time for Joe to wake up and get busy in the kitchen.

We kept this event to ourselves, often second guessing our summation, thinking that eventually something was going to pop up and give us a perfectly logical explanation. I think it is human nature to question these types of things, and important for people to realize *we questioned them plenty*. Ryan must have been frustrated with our ambivalence, because he used the scent of bacon again a few weeks later on another family member...

My mother-in-law had to have several heart stints put in, and after the procedure we brought her to our home to recover for a few days. She slept in our bedroom during her stay. It was a Sunday morning when she came into the living room where Joe and I were enjoying our morning coffee. "Oh," she said, "I thought you were cooking breakfast. The smell of bacon woke me up." My husband and I just looked at each other, speechless. Then I started to laugh with glee! Ryan was using grandma this time to make sure his message clear. There was no second guessing after that. Bacon in the master bedroom = Ryan saying hello. We got it!

It was also about this time that I experienced a few strange occurrences involving our telephone. I was in Ryan's room one day, my head in his drawer, sobbing and smelling his things. I'd let myself get sucked into the black hole and I was having quite a time getting out. Eventually I forced myself to sit up, catch my breath, and blow my nose. I was lowering my head back into his drawer when I heard the phone ring. I sat upright, and tried to decide if I wanted to answer it or not. It took a moment to pull myself together, but I managed to answer on the 5th or 6th ring.

I put the receiver to my ear and said, "Hello," but there was nothing but static on the other end. I repeated my greeting several times, but never got a response. Puzzled, I stayed on the line. I waited for a dial tone, thinking the call had been disconnected, but the static continued to crackle loudly in my ear. I held on a little longer, and then finally hung up. I went upstairs to check our caller ID. No number was listed. It was as if the call had never taken place. These "static calls" happened several times that summer, and they always happened while I was alone — in the black hole. Nothing but static and no name listed on the caller ID. Was this Ryan's way of getting me to stop crying? The thought of this possibility comforted me, and so I simply let it be.

In the midst of our anguish, these little points of contact were bright sparks in the darkness that kept our hope alive. It was apparent however, that we could not spend the rest of our lives just hanging around waiting for Ryan to contact us. We needed a diversion from all this grief. The answer to our dilemma wasn't far behind this realization. Katie and I found it a week or so later at the local dog pound, in the form of a mutt that we named Maxx.

It was a sunny day in late July and we had spent the morning walking each and every aisle at the Humane Society looking for a new pet. We didn't have any luck there, so we called my husband for some help. He suggested that we drive across town to the dog pound — so we did. We tramped through that whole facility too, and were about to give up on the idea when we saw a puppy sitting at the back of his cage, head down, and quivering. We pressed our noses to the cage and tried coaxing him forward so we could pet him.

The man showing us around asked if we wanted to hold him. We nodded in agreement. He opened the cage, and when Katie reached out to him, he came forward and climbed into her arms. Maxx put one paw on each side of her neck and laid his little head on her shoulder. That was all it took. Katie turned to me and said, "Mom, please go pay for my puppy."

Without a doubt, this dog was ours. The man smiled and told us that yesterday this puppy had been scheduled for euthanasia since he was already about 3 months old, but something had made the dog pound employee change his mind. He had decided to give the puppy another week to see if he could find him a home. It made us happy to think we had saved his life, but in truth it was Maxx who was about to save ours.

If anyone were to ask me for advice on how to help a family deal with grief, I would have to say — get a dog. Maxx got us over more humps than I can even begin to count. We poured our displaced affection for

Ryan into our puppy. In return, he gave us all protection, laughter and unconditional love. Maxx brought joy back into the house. Caring for him helped us focus our attention on something other than our sadness and that made him worth his weight in gold.

Because I was off work for so long, he became "mine." We spent every minute of every day together. When I couldn't seem to get out of bed, he would simply join me. If he found me crying, he gently licked off my tears. Sometimes I would wail out loud and Maxx took this as an invitation to chime right in. His beagle genes made it natural for him to howl right along with me. This always made me laugh, which pleased him greatly.

It was evident from the start that Ryan loved Maxx too. Our dog gave him many great opportunities to communicate with us. Pets have an advantage over humans because they can see and hear spirits. Ryan has used Maxx many times over the years to help him — help us.

The first time this happened Maxx had only been with us for a few days. We were sitting on the deck, and he was laying at our feet relaxing and soaking up the sun. Suddenly Maxx lifted his head, and leapt off the deck. Going full speed, he began racing around the pool. He had made about three laps around when Katie turned to me and said, "He's chasing Ryan." This made sense. It was clear that Maxx was in pursuit of something. This happened several times that summer. It is just a small example of the many things they did, and continue to do, which sharpens our awareness and lightens our load.

Maxx was a great diversion, and we needed that. I am mostly grateful for how he managed to help Katie. She calls Maxx her "doggie man" and from day one, she was his "sissy." He is fiercely protective of her and this quality alone was enough to help her move back into her bedroom in the lower level. Each night they would descend the stairs together, with Maxx leading the way. He began sleeping on her bed every night. Katie loved and needed this. Cuddling and playing with him helped to nurse her pain which was something she had not been able to let any of the rest of us do. This more than made up for every shoe, bra, and deck board Maxx chewed up and destroyed over the next few years. His love was magic, and the best part was that we had access to him 24/7.

Our dog, Maxx

7

THE THREE MONTH MARKER

I HAD MAXX TO help me pass the time, but he could do nothing for the pain and longing I held inside of me. The contact Ryan had given us was wonderful, but I could not fathom that anything short of touching the real thing was going to be able to help me with this hunger I could not seem to curb. The yearning to see and hold my son became a chronic ache, and with each passing day, it was becoming more unbearable. Without a doubt, *the loss of physical touch is the cruelest part of grief.*

You would think that having my daughter would be enough to get me over this hump. I will tell you that having her to hold is a tremendous source of comfort. Only God knows the true magnitude of my love for Katie, and the gratitude I feel every time I look at her or touch her. However, the simple fact of this matter is that you can never replace the love you feel for one child with another. Had the situation been reversed, I would feel no differently. Inside I knew that somewhere, somehow, I had to find a way to pacify this yearning or run the risk of completely losing my mind.

The little things that we experienced at home were all due to Ryan contacting us. I felt at a loss because I had no idea of how to contact him. I knew it was possible because that was what Elaine had done for me, but I was hesitant to call on her again for this purpose. I did not want to become dependent on the readings. I discussed this with my husband. Joe just wanted me to feel better, so he encouraged me to go again if I thought it would help me. His support was all I needed. After

weeks of pondering, I decided to call Elaine for another reading.

We were heading into our third month of grieving when the second reading took place. I was excited and beyond ready to touch base with Ryan when I arrived at Elaine's. Within moments, I found myself perched on the edge of a chair, pen and paper in hand. I sat patiently as I waited for her to begin.

She was surprised that Ryan was so eager to communicate. She told me that her experience had been that suicides were generally hard to make contact with; they were reluctant due to their shame or remorse — but Ryan was an exception. His energy was strong and he was anxious to converse with me. This made me realize how lucky I was, and I felt grateful.

Ryan started by discussing my dad. They had a very close relationship, much like father and son, and my dad was suffering terribly from the loss of him. He wanted Grandpa to know that the suicide wasn't his fault in any way, and that he understood that my dad had just been trying to help him. He thanked his grandpa for this and for his "financial support". My dad and Ryan were always wheeling and dealing. Ryan knew he could always count on Grandpa when he needed help with his "get rich quick" schemes. To Ryan's credit, he always made sure he paid my dad back. I knew this message would mean a lot to him.

"Tell your dad to check the left rear tire on the tractor. Ryan keeps saying it needs to be fixed," Elaine added. Later, when I told my dad this, he shook his head and started to laugh. "That little shit," he said, "He knows that tire is a bugger. It took the both of us almost two months to pull that thing off the first time." My dad loved that tidbit, because that tire had been a private joke between the two of them. Ryan had carefully selected a detail that would assure his grandpa that he was watching over him too.

He showed Elaine a yellow rose. That week, I had cut a yellow rose from one of my bushes and had taken it to the cemetery for him. Ryan also acknowledged my working in the flowerbeds. The perennials by the pool had become congested and I had forced myself outside to dig some of them up. "Oh," she said, "he's patting you on the back." It appeared that my gardening had made him proud of me. Actually, I had been proud of myself, because it was the most activity I'd been capable of since the funeral.

Ryan now felt sorry about the suicide and expressed his regret. He had told me in the first reading that he "would do it again." It appeared that watching us grieve for the past three months had changed his mind about that. He made it a point to tell me that his disappointment in life had not come from me. "You gave your all Mom," he told me.

Switching gears, Elaine asked, "Do you have a special ring?" I did not. She explained that this was probably something for the future. Then she asked if I had more than one earring in one ear. Ha! I did have one ear that was double pierced, but I hadn't worn an earring in it for years. I was impressed that Ryan remembered that, and had thought to use it to validate his presence.

I was ready this time when Elaine asked me if I had any questions. I asked Ryan "Where can you hear me? Where should I go if I want to make sure you are listening?" She was still for a moment and then said, "Under the big tree." Immediately I thought of the tree at the cemetery. I had been spending a lot of time talking out loud to him there. I had specifically picked a plot for him under a tree because he hated to be hot. This tree provided a nice shady spot, and I was glad to know that he had seen me there.

Knowing this triggered something deep inside of me, and I began to weep. I told him "Ryan — I can't do this. I can't make it without you...It's just too hard!" I let my anguish spill from me, as poor Elaine sat there in silence. When I regained my composure, she looked at me with compassion and softly said, "He wants you to know that *you can* do this. He's telling me — I'll help you Mom." I tried to take comfort in his words, but didn't see how he was going to be capable of that.

The reading was over. I stood up and prepared to leave. Suddenly, Elaine reached for my hand and said, "Wait — He's giving me something else. What does *Jack and the Beanstalk* mean to you?"

Everything — IT MEANT EVERYTHING. *Jack in the Beanstalk* was something only Ryan could possibly know. I had mentioned it at the cemetery the day before. I had gone there alone to sink a plaque I'd purchased into the ground in front of his headstone. The plaque says, "If tears could make a stairway and memories a lane, I'd walk right up to heaven and bring you home again." I had read this to him aloud, as I placed the plaque into the soil. I told him, "Yep Ryan — just like *Jack and the Beanstalk* — I'd climb up there, get you, and never let you go."

This validation ensured that he could most definitely hear me if I was "Under the big tree." Now, I knew that anything important I had to communicate could be said there, and I took comfort in knowing that Ryan would be listening. This meant that now I did not have to depend on the readings to contact him.

I hugged Elaine and thanked her for the peace of mind our time together had given me. It had definitely lifted my spirits and the intensity of my grief had been drastically reduced. I had reached out to Ryan for help and he had handed me a big juicy hook. Fabulous! It felt so good — to feel so good — I hummed the rest of the way home.

8

RYAN'S HELPING HAND

"I'LL HELP YOU MOM," is the promise Ryan made to me. I knew my son — he would never say this to me if it weren't so. I vowed to keep myself open; I did not want to miss anything he managed to send my way. The healing power of his contact was too valuable to waste. I was headed homeward, completely clueless to the fact that a windfall of activity was about to take place.

I drove into town after the reading to do a few errands. My first stop was at the pharmacy to get a few prescriptions filled. I went inside and spent some time looking at the greeting cards as I waited for my refills. I live in a small town and many people were aware of what had happened to Ryan. I discussed it openly. I was not ashamed of my son and found no reason to lie about the fact that it had been suicide. In fact, I made a slight reference to it as I stood at the register to pay. I said, "I can't help but wonder that if Ryan had taken an anti-depressant, would he be here today?" Our pharmacist is very kind, and he responded by saying that, "In some cases, it doesn't always make a difference."

I thanked him for his comforting words and waved goodbye as I headed out the door. I had only taken a few steps toward my vehicle when I heard someone call my name. I turned and realized that one of the girls who worked there had followed me outside. She asked me if I had just a minute or two as she had something she wanted to tell me. I turned toward her, and gave her my full attention.

"I tried to take my life once," she told me. "I think it is important for you to know that when someone makes up their mind to do it, there isn't anything anyone can do to stop them. It's like having blinders on, because you can't see or hear anything beyond your own pain. All you can think about is finding peace. I just thought you should know that, because I'm sure your son doesn't want you to feel guilty about what happened. It didn't have anything to do with you — it was him, his feelings, his choice, his decision..."

I could hardly believe my ears. All I could think of was *Ryan, Ryan, Ryan,* and the words he had given me less than an hour ago — "I'll help you Mom." I looked at her and said, "All I can do is to try and understand. Your words and insight have been very helpful. Thank you so much for sharing your story. I'm sure that was not easy for you to do." I reached out and gave her a big hug.

She hugged me back and told me she had wanted to share this with me for awhile, but the timing had just never seemed right. "I don't know what made me do it today!" she said. I did, but I kept that to myself. We talked a few minutes longer and then she went back inside. I got into the car and drove to the grocery store continuing with my errands.

I was sure this was Ryan trying to help me. What were the chances that today of all days, that young woman would choose to tell me such a personal story? I barely knew her…All I could do was take it in and try to process it all. I was doing exactly that as I walked toward the entrance of the grocery store. At the entry, I recognized a woman I had spoken to at the funeral. She was the mother of one of Katie's friends. At the funeral home, in an effort to comfort me, she had shared a personal story with me regarding the loss of her brother. She smiled as we approached one another.

"How are you doing?" she asked me. I said I was doing alright and asked how her day was going. She told me she was having a good day and was glad she'd run into me because she had a little story she wanted to tell me. Evidently her brother's birthday had just passed. It had been a beautiful day she told me — sunny and calm. She had spent some time working in her garden that afternoon, thinking of him and talking to him. She was heading back into the house when all of a sudden her wind chime started to make noise. She turned around to look at it, curious because the air had been completely still, however the wind chime was gently swaying, to and fro, playing its beautiful music. "I knew it was him," she told me "He was just saying hello."

I loved this story for two reasons. First, it made me feel less crazy to know other people got "signs" like this too. Secondly, I don't believe in coincidence. The fact that I'd just had two conversations in the last 15 minutes relating to both suicide and spirit contact was incredible! I could barely contain my excitement and decided to share with her that I had been getting little signs from Ryan also.

She hugged me and told me to embrace those signs, that she believed in them and so should I. Thrilled beyond words at how my day was rolling along, I smiled, and thanked her for sharing her beautiful story. We parted and I went inside to get my groceries.

An hour later, I was finally in my car heading for home. I was reaching over to turn the CD player on when "I Need You," by LeAnn Rimes started to play on the radio. Instantly, my eyes filled with tears. The day Ryan died I could not get this song out of my head. Every time it plays, I think of him. The lyrics express exactly how I feel. This was a wonderful way to validate that he was indeed there — helping me.

When this happened to my family, I could not help but wonder how we would ever be able to live in a world where he wasn't. But I was beginning to realize that wasn't going to be the case, because from day one, Ryan had made it very clear that a part of him was still here. In truth, his spirit had never left us. I could hardly wait to tell Katie and Joe about my day. I entered the house with a huge smile on my face, thinking "Crazy or not — here I come."

9

COMPANY IN HELL

RYAN'S HELP WAS EXACTLY what I'd needed. I could feel his love—reaching out to me. This refueled my spirit and kept me pushing forward. I had hoped that sharing my experience with Joe and Katie would have given them the same feeling. But it is one thing to experience something directly, and quite another to hear about it second hand. I soon realized that there wasn't going to be a "cure all" remedy for our pain, but still believed that we could all benefit by sharing our hope.

What helped me most was to stay focused on the fact that I was still a wife and mother. I knew that Joe and Katie needed me and this knowledge was what kept me going hour by hour. What little energy I could muster was focused on my family; everything else took a back seat to their needs. I tried to keep our household running, but struggled daily to get the most ordinary of tasks completed.

I was spending much of my time alone and this provided too many opportunities to dwell on past events. All too often, these thoughts would hurl me into the black hole, where I could feel the intensity of my grief cresting on the borders of insanity. It is hard to explain what it feels like to be locked inside of your pain. For me, it felt as if I were sitting in a boat, drifting aimlessly down a river. On both sides of me were tall, mountainous walls of stone. I felt that one side represented my past, the other my future; I was trapped there between them — unable to go back, and too overwhelmed to move forward.

Ryan's death had immobilized my father, in much of the same way it had me. He is the type of person who is generally "on the go". Dad has a lot of friends and they tried to keep him busy, but he ended up spending most of that first summer sitting in his lawn chair, under the shade trees near his barn or in the garage at the house.

Ryan had loved spending time with his grandpa. From the day he was born, until the day he died, he and my father had been joined at the hip. Ryan helped him with anything and everything. They shared the same love for trucks, tractors and bulldozers — of which my dad had several. Dad taught him how to work on engines and they refurbished a tractor or two together. Watching him without Ryan was like watching a man try to walk with only one leg. It was painful to see my father suffer so, but despite everything he had to deal with, he chose to respect my loss first, and gave me the steadying hand I so desperately needed.

Most every morning he would stop at our house to check up on me. He'd come in through the back gate by the pool, knowing he'd find me there sitting on the deck, staring into space. On one such occasion, he walked up to me and said; "Only one of us is allowed to be in hell at a time, and today is my turn." I think I managed to give him a little smile that day, but what I remember most was how good it felt to hear him say I hadn't been there alone. If I had to be in hell, at least I was in good company.

It had been Dad's idea to bury Ryan's ashes at the cemetery. After the funeral, he'd asked what we were planning to do with them. I told him we hadn't really thought about it, and asked if he had any ideas. His only request was that we please keep all of Ryan's ashes together; he then suggested getting a plot at the cemetery for them. I liked Dad's idea and that was exactly what we did. The cemetery is only a few miles down the same road that we all live on. Having the ashes there kept Ryan close to home and we all liked that. It was the right thing to do. It gave us all somewhere to go when we wanted to be with him; a place where we could privately mourn.

I didn't know how to help my father. I was too broken to offer him much of anything, except an ear to listen and someone to cry with when he needed to. We kept close tabs on each other, and were just kind of drifting along when a miracle came out of nowhere.

My brother David called to tell us that he and his wife Kim were going to have a baby. This was fantastic news! They had waited a long time for a child, and at one point, weren't even sure they were going to be able to have a family. My dad was especially excited. My brother is the only boy in our family of six (he was raised with my two sisters and me), and we were all secretly hoping they'd have a son to carry on the family name. Knowing the stork was on its way gave us all a big lift, which was something we desperately needed.

Dad and I carried a huge load of grief for Ryan, but my husband's burden was much bigger than ours was. Joe had a horrendous year, one that was heavily marked with death. His father passed away in February, Ryan died in June, and in October, his dearest friend and hunting buddy, Sinbad, suddenly passed away. To say that Joe was overcome with sorrow would be a gross understatement. Each death in itself had been a crushing blow, with little time in between to do any type of real healing.

It was the first time I realized how strong my husband really was. He had to be in order to keep his emotions in check the way he did that year. He quietly carried his grief around inside of him. There were only a few occasions where Joe allowed me to see the weight of the burden he bore. Those circumstances were usually prompted by my emotional breakdowns. Joe was very supportive, but seeing me cry was a huge trigger for him. His reaction was to get very angry with Ryan. "I can't stand to see what his actions have done to us," he'd tell me. All the needless pain the suicide had created gave Joe something to direct his anguish at, and no one could really blame him for that.

I was concerned for Joe and my father, but I worried about Katie the most. She was the epitome of anger, and refused to accept any help as she struggled with her grief. After the suicide, Katie wouldn't talk about her brother or her feelings. She put up a wall around herself that none of us could penetrate. I switched therapists for her twice, but after only a few months, she balked about continuing. Our doctor prescribed medication to help with her anxiety, but Katie was still easily agitated. I could not force her to seek help. I kept a watchful eye on her and waited patiently for her to come to me.

The holidays that year were especially difficult for my daughter, and I believe the stress of the season is what finally forced her to confront her loss. It was on Thanksgiving Day that she finally reached a breaking point...

We'd had dinner at my mother-in-law's that day, and then went to see my Aunt Kat and the family she had gathered at her home. Our plans were to have a short visit with them, then go to the movies. My cousin Cindi was there, and on a whim I invited her son, Mikey, to come along and see *Santa Clause 2* with us. I thought it would be more fun to bring a younger child along. In truth, it was easier to do things in the company of others. When it was just the three of us, we were all too conscious of the fact that something was missing.

Throughout the movie, I watched as Mikey pointed and whispered things into Katie's ear. As the evening progressed, I noticed her demeanor change from stoic to sorrowful. The banter between them proved to be all too familiar for Katie. It had triggered memories of her brother, and I could see that she was struggling to keep her emotions under wraps. I watched as she sucked it up, her eyes fixed on the movie screen, determined not to give in to them. She managed to maintain her resolve for the duration of the movie, but it didn't last for long.

Later that evening, Katie came into our bedroom where I was busy getting ready for bed. As she walked toward me, I could clearly see that the walls were tumbling down around her. I rushed to meet her, and quickly enfolded Katie into my arms. I held my daughter close to me, gently rubbing her back as she released a flood of unshed tears. Later, we sat together on the bed and I listened as she explained to me how for the past six months she'd been pretending that Ryan was on vacation. She said, "I realized tonight that my brother isn't coming home."

I embraced my daughter protectively. I longed to strip the pain from her body and make her world right again, but that wasn't possible — the damage had been done. All I could do was love her, and let her know I was there for her. It was a relief to know that the door grief had built between us was finally open.

My dad, Joe, Katie and I were all fighting to maintain the armor we had so carefully encased ourselves in, trying to protect our shattered lives from further destruction. In order to heal we were going to have to ditch that armor and feel the pain associated with letting go. The world we once knew was gone; we were going to have to break out in order to break free and move beyond the suicide. Understanding this was a big step, but not one we were ready to take — at least not yet.

HOPE YOU CAN HOLD

MY BROTHER'S BABY WASN'T due until spring. David and Kim live in Atlanta, so we spent a fair amount of time on the telephone and swapping e-mails to get updates on her pregnancy. During one such phone conversation, my brother brought up the impending holiday season. I told him I had gone to a grieving seminar and that they had instructed us to "have a plan" for every holiday or celebratory occasion.

I'd had a plan for Thanksgiving, but didn't really know what we were going to do about Christmas. A week or so later David called back and asked if we would like to spend Christmas with them in Atlanta. Getting out of town seemed like a good idea. We all needed a change of scenery, and this provided the perfect opportunity. I thanked David and took him up on his offer.

My sister-in-law Kim is what I refer to as an "earth angel." Right from day one, she had jumped in and done everything she could to help us, as did David. She handed us cleverly constructed itineraries when we arrived at their home that Christmas. They had taken to heart what I had said about "having a plan," and our schedule was filled with things for us to enjoy during the holiday.

Our first outing was to an Atlanta Falcons football game, followed by a visit to Centennial Park, which was brightly lit and beautifully decorated for the holidays. Over the next several days, we made trips to the Coke museum, CNN studios, and the home of author Margaret Mitchell. Each day was an adventure, designed to keep our bodies moving and our minds occupied.

On Christmas Eve, after we were all in bed, we heard a loud "kaboom." It awoke both Joe and I, and we joked that maybe my brother had fallen out of bed. The next morning we looked outside and discovered that one of the huge Georgia pines in their yard had toppled over. The massive tree had slightly brushed the back of their house. The only damage had been to an eaves trough. It lay on the ground next to the screened-in porch. Clearly, a guardian angel had been watching over us all.

Later that morning, we were in the kitchen discussing the fallen tree when my brother suddenly pointed out the window. There in his driveway were hundreds of birds, and I do mean hundreds. As we looked on, the entire flock took off in flight. It was one of the most peculiar, yet fascinating things I had ever seen. I remember locking eyes with my brother when this happened. He experienced something at that moment too, but neither of us has ever been able to describe it.

Christmas was soon over and we were reluctant to go home. Staying busy had kept us from being preoccupied with our sadness, and the change in location proved to be helpful too. We didn't have the expectation of seeing Ryan at their house, as we would have expected to see him at home. This trip verified that having a plan was important. So when we got back home, we focused on our strategy for New Year's Eve. Katie decided to spend it with a few of her friends. Joe and I got a small group together and we made reservations to attend a party at the Country Club.

On New Year's Eve, we had a few couples meet at our house for cocktails before heading out to the party. Katie visited with our friends and took pictures of us in front the Christmas tree before she headed out for the evening. It felt a little strange to be going to a party, but we were surrounded by good friends and they were unwavering in their mission to help us enjoy the evening.

January arrived and the holidays were officially over. I made a trip to the local drug store and dropped off several rolls of film to be developed. I picked our pictures up the following day and decided to look at them while sitting in the parking lot. I was halfway through the stack when I noticed something unusual about one of the pictures. It was a photo of Joe and me, taken in front of the Christmas tree on New Year's Eve.

Milky white fingers of light splayed across the entire right side of the picture, in a form that closely resembled the edge of an angel's wing. You could see our faces right through the image, because it was somewhat transparent. A second picture had been taken of us in the same pose, within seconds of the first, but the second photo did not have the fingers of light in it. In fact, there wasn't any other picture in the whole stack that looked like that one. I felt my heart skip a beat. I had read about "spirit light" pictures, and prayed that I was holding one.

I hurried home to show Katie and Joe. They also agreed that it looked just like the edge of an angel's wing (Elaine verified this for me later in another reading), and we took this as a sign that Ryan had visited us for the holiday. It was a belated Christmas gift for us all.

This picture was a real, solid, physical object, and proof that something special was indeed happening to us. The best part was that it gave us something to hold and share with others. Battling our own personal doubts about the remarkable things we were experiencing was still a challenge, but in this case having evidence made it easier to believe. I kept our picture close to me and thanked Ryan for the priceless present he had sent our way. When it came to giving a gift, he was never the type to be outdone. It was great to know that some things never change.

The Reason

Our first Spirit Light picture, Christmas 2002

PART TWO

A NEW FOUNDATION

11

RELATIONSHIPS

AT THE SIX MONTH mark, I could see that we were making some head-way in our battle through grief, but they were baby steps to be sure. Slowly our lives had begun to change as we responded to our new situation. As we evolved, so did our relationships; not only with each other, but with most everyone we knew. Death creates a ripple effect and this was just one of the several circumstances in which we could see it.

I read somewhere that thirty percent of the marriages that experience the loss of a child end in divorce. I am happy that we are not in that percentile. Ryan's death brought Joe and I closer together. We had many opportunities to turn on each other, but we chose not to let that happen. We needed each other — of that we were sure — and I believe it was our saving grace. We didn't blame each other; we listened to one another and both agreed that Katie's welfare was our number one priority.

Joe is the stepfather, and although my children loved and respect-ed him, they weren't always as close as they could have been. He would often step back, putting me in charge of discipline and the many other decisions regarding their welfare. Joe did not feel that he had the right to make those choices. After the suicide, we formed a much tighter fam-ily unit and he became more active in his parenting role. Katie reaped the benefits from this change and grew closer to Joe because of it. She began trusting him more and this helped to ease some of the anxieties she was experiencing.

Trust and kindness are key in any good relationship, and in the wake of the suicide, we used these qualities to help determine who our true friends and caring relatives were. We never anticipated having to re-evaluate our relationships, but the startling behavior we experienced at the funeral and in the days that followed caused us to do so. Death had reminded us that life was short, and it was far too short to waste our valuable time on people who didn't warrant it. This included the people who:

✓ Avoided us as if losing a child was a contagious dis-ease — they stood back from us both physically and emotionally as if they were going to "catch" suicide.

✓ Just wanted to pretend that nothing had happened and completely avoided any conversation regarding Ryan or our loss; these were the "get over it" and "life goes on" people.

✓ Were friends from our past that we hadn't seen in years; they showed up at the funeral merely to gawk and collect gossip.

✓ Came to appease their guilt — We couldn't get their help when we'd needed it most, and after the fact, it was too little — too late.

We had some pleasant surprises too. These were:

✓ Friends from the past who re-entered our lives and some people on the "fringe" of our world that moved in closer by making their contact more frequent and meaningful.
✓ The new friends we made with several other parents that

had also lost a child. These friendships proved to be price-less because no one else in the world understands how you feel better than they do.

Our "core" friends, for the most part, never skipped a beat when it came to giving us their time, love and support. Throughout the ordeal of the suicide, and in the months and years since, they have stuck by us faithfully. We learned many valuable things about our friends and ourselves during this difficult time and for that, I will always be thankful.

My friend Tammy started sending me cards and helpful books soon after hearing of Ryan's death. She did that for well over two years. To this day, she never forgets his birthday or his death date; she always takes the time to give me a call or send a card. Nothing is more healing or appreciated than to have your child remembered on those crucial dates. Tammy's thoughtful acts taught me *the importance of remembering*. I will always be grateful to her for reaching out to me, and for teaching me something I continue to practice — sending cards of remembrance to others whose lives have also been touched by grief.

On the evening of the suicide, my friend Lori came to our house to console me. I will never forget how comforting it was to have her there. We cried together, and she gave me support when I needed it most. She did not shy away from the tragic circumstances that confronted me; instead, she created a wall of love for me to lean on and acted as my shield in the days and months that followed. Lori's actions taught me the *importance of loyalty*. Because of her, I understand the value of being there, listening without judgment, and the significance of time spent with friends who really care about you.

It is strange how the smallest of actions become so large in your memory. When it comes to the funeral, and the months that followed, it is the people and how they treated us that I will probably remember

best. Good, bad, or indifferent, their actions and reactions to our situation played a formidable part in the reconstruction of our lives.

Tragedy does have a positive side in that it removes the clutter and crap from your life. After it strikes, you have a clearer understanding of what and who is important to you. This makes everything much simpler, and at this point — simple was all we could do.

THE STORK DELIVERS

EARLY IN MARCH, I received a call from my sister-in-law Kim. She was driving herself to the hospital because she was experiencing discomfort and felt that something wasn't right. My brother was on a church retreat somewhere in a park in Georgia. Knowing how resourceful I can often be, she called to tell me the situation and asked me to find David and have him come to the hospital. She had tried to contact him, but he was in the mountains and his cell phone wasn't working.

I was sitting in Michigan, but you can bet I didn't argue this fact with her. All I knew was that she needed help and had designated me to get the job done. I reassured her that everything would be alright, and got to work hunting down my brother. Kim had given me the name of the park where the retreat was taking place, so I looked it up online and luckily found a telephone number to call. I couldn't believe it when someone actually answered the phone, because it was a general information number and a Sunday. I explained the situation to the park ranger who answered, and he assured me he would locate my brother.

David called back in less than 10 minutes. I calmly explained that Kim was fine, but was going to the hospital to get checked out and needed him to join her there as soon as possible. "I can't believe you found me," was all David could say, and then he was on his way.

Kim stayed overnight at the hospital and the next day it was decided that the baby needed to be born. This made the delivery ahead of schedule, which created some concerns, but the benefits outweighed the risks and that afternoon their baby boy (James Alexander) was born. I told them not to worry, because I was sending my personal angel down to keep watch over their precious baby.

Later that same day, I had an interesting conversation with my brother. David called me from his house; he'd made a quick trip home to change and freshen up. He told me that both Kim and Alex were doing fine, and then asked if I remembered telling him about the angel I had sent to watch over Alex. When I acknowledged that I did, he proceeded to tell me about the buck in his backyard.

David said it was there waiting for him when he got home. He pulled into his driveway, and saw it standing there, quietly staring at his house. He said it reminded him of the buck at our parent's house that previous summer, and this had convinced him that it was a sign from my son. "I feel like Ryan is telling me not to worry, that he's here, watching over Alex just like you asked him to do." My brother's voice broke a little and in the silence that followed, I know that tears were quietly being shed.

I quickly recalled a story my dad had told me about a large buck that had suddenly started to appear right after Ryan died. Each morning, he would look out the window and see it standing there in the cornfield looking at their house, as if it were keeping guard. Dad didn't say that it was Ryan, but I could tell by the way he told the story that he felt as if it were...

This was a happy day for my brother, and I wanted it to remain that way, so to lighten the mood, I found my voice and said, "Well, it's good to know I can still give Ryan orders." This made us both laugh and that felt good. Our conversation soon ended and David headed back up to the hospital to spend time with his family.

Alex benefited from the special care he received at the hospital and was soon home, breaking his parents in. At his christening later that same year, I got my second spirit light picture. It was a thrill to get it, and to know that Ryan continues to watch over my nephew. I see two miracles when I look at that picture, and thank God everyday — for both of them.

Ryan continues to watch over his cousin Alex
(Spirit Light on Grandma's right shoulder at Alex's Christening)

13

BARRIE AND JUDIE

I WENT BACK TO work in January of 2003, six months after the suicide. It was a new job, in a new facility and I was ready for the change. The best part of going back to work for me was being around people again. I focused on learning my new job and making friends. I had been nervous about taking the position and had asked Ryan for a sign. I knew I was in the right place, when I discovered the exchange on my office telephone (3187) was almost the same as the exchange at home (3817). This seemed like a good sign to me!

Having my time occupied in a more constructive manner helped ease me through the days. In respect to time itself, I noticed that I had begun marking time by Ryan's death date. Every time the 28th rolled around I would count backward and think, "He's been gone six (seven, eight, nine, etc) months. I also did this when describing dates related to certain events or holidays, thinking that they happened before or after Ryan died. Keeping time this way distinguished for me the separation of my life in halves; one half with — and the other half without — my son.

We were 9 months into the first year of mourning when I received a phone call at work from Rosalie. She was the receptionist for our chiropractor, and is a delight to know. She called to tell me that mutual friends of ours, Barrie and Judie, had just received the news that their daughter Angie had been killed in a plane accident. She had immediately thought of me and wondered if I could help them in any way.

I knew all too well how important it was to have immediate support, but wasn't sure of the best way to approach them. It was mid-April, and we were scheduled to leave on vacation the following day, which meant we were going to miss the funeral. Waiting until after vacation to contact them was *not* an option, so I decided that for now, a phone call would have to do. When I made the call, I got their answering machine. I chose my words carefully knowing what a difficult day it was for them.

I began the message by telling them about our travel plans, including the date of our return. It was important for them to know why we weren't going to be at the funeral. When it came to offering words of comfort, I simply looked back in time, remembering what had made me feel better and spoke from my heart. I said, "This is going to be the hardest day of your life, but I want you to know you are going to be okay. We are here for you and will help you both in any way we can." I encouraged them to call us as soon as they felt up to it, and reaffirmed that we would soon be in touch. I got very choked up, but managed to finish my message. It was with a heavy heart that we all left for vacation.

A week after our return, Judie called me up. I will never forget the first words she spoke to me, she said "Sal, is it always going to hurt this much?" I knew all too well how she was feeling...that crushing pain and longing — so fresh, so raw. I wanted to give her hope, but I wasn't going to lie to her either. I told her that although it never goes away, it did in fact get a little bit easier to tolerate with each passing day. This was an epiphany for me, because until that moment I had not thought to compare where she was, in relationship to where I currently stood. Her question had given me cause to look back, and it was a relief to know that I had indeed made some progress.

We spoke for quite some time. It was such a relief to me to be able to speak in truth everything I was feeling without holding back. It hadn't even been a year, but I found myself giving her guidance, reassurance, and hope. For me, it was huge to be able to do this for another human being. It was what I had hoped for in the earliest days of my mourning, someone to talk to who knew what it felt like to suddenly be caught in the jaws of grief. I only had my own experiences to share, but for Judie it was enough. I was devastated by the circumstances that had brought us closer together, but at the same time grateful to have someone with whom to share these things.

Judie owned a massage therapy business in town. In the past, she'd given me massages and we would see each other occasionally, but it wasn't until we lost our children that we became close friends. She and I made it a point to get together for lunch when we could and spent a lot of time on the telephone coaching one another through difficult days.

Barrie is just as friendly and as easy to be with as Judie, and soon we were getting together as couples. It was a huge benefit to have another couple to talk with, but it didn't stop there. With all the talk about "Barrie and Judie" at home, Katie was soon joining us for dinners out and our "gab fests." They quickly became our extended family and strongest allies as we worked to rebuild our lives.

Tragedy brought us together, but the love that grew between us created a bond that we will always share. Joe, Katie and I are truly blessed to know these warm and gracious people. They helped us to see that there was a light at the end of the tunnel. We banded together, and inched our way toward it.

Barrie and Judie's daughter, Angie LaClair
05/30/68 – 4/13/03

BIRDS OF A FEATHER

THE MORE TIME I spent with Barrie and Judie, the more I realized how very much we had in common. Like me, they both loved to read. Soon we were swapping books and sharing our thoughts on philosophy and spirituality. It was truly a gift to be able to share my ideas and opinions with like minded people. The best by-product of this was the way we began to slowly shift our focus away from our losses to a more positive way of thinking and living.

I have always been interested in astrology, the afterlife, and reincarnation. I feel now that there was a reason for my interest in them so early in life. My knowledge was limited in these subjects before Ryan's death, but the small amount I had retained was enough to open my heart and mind. Without that, I would have found myself completely unarmed and unable to cope with the heartbreaking circumstances that befell me. It felt natural to turn to these topics for help as I searched for the answers to my questions. I had read quite a few books by the time Judie and Barrie entered the picture, and I felt confident suggesting a few to help them when I discovered how similar our tastes were.

Here are several books I found to be particularly helpful and recommended to them:

✓ *Life after Life* by Raymond A. Moody, Jr., M.D.

✓ *Talking to Heaven* by James Van Praagh

✓ *The Celestine Prophecy* by James Redfield

The Reason

- ✓ *Why Bad Things Happen to Good People* by Harold S. Kushner

- ✓ *After Life* by John Edward

- ✓ *The Afterlife Experiments* by Gary E. Schwartz, Ph.D. with William L. Simon

- ✓ *Journey of Souls* by Michael Newton, Ph.D.

- ✓ *The Tibetan Book of Living and Dying* by Sogyal Rinpoche

In return, Judie and Barrie shared several of their audio tapes by Dr. Wayne Dyer, and Dr. David Hawkins. They also introduced me to the writing of Deepak Chopra. Judie bought *The Seven Spiritual Laws of Success* for me, and several years later both she and I had our copies of this book signed by Deepak at one of his lectures. This was especially meaningful for Judie because her daughter Angie had purchased her copy.

Barrie and Judie are much more knowledgeable than I am in respect to understanding and applying the thoughts and ideas of these books and their authors. During our discussions, they would take the time to answer my questions and freely shared their ideas which helped me to better comprehend and relate to the new world I found myself discovering. This encouraged me to explore my beliefs further and for the first time, I felt comfortable discussing and embracing my spirituality.

I also shared with them what I began to refer to as "miracles" — those little signs Ryan had been sending our way. The dictionary defines a miracle as, "...an extraordinary event manifesting divine intervention in human affairs..." which was exactly what we had been experiencing. They found this to be very exciting and never questioned our sanity. In fact, once that door was opened, they were anxious to share a few of their miracles with us.

Judie told me that Angie had contacted her, by actually speaking to her (telepathically), the day after the plane crash. She said that they had gone to the doctor that morning because Barrie had experienced chest pains the evening before. The doctor eased their minds some by telling them it had been a reaction to the severe stress that the news of Angie's death had brought on, and then he'd sent them home. The following is Judie's recollection of that morning:

"…Back home, I stood on our deck, lost in the deepest pain of my grief. I was thinking about the fire from the plane crash, and wondering — did she suffer? My God! How can I live knowing our cherished daughter may have died in agony? I'm not sure how long I was standing out there. Suddenly I heard in my head, "What's the big deal Mom?" I gasped, and said, "Angie?!"

Angie said, "It's O.K. Mom, it didn't hurt!" She continued, "Grandpa is right here with me — Don't cry Mom! Open your heart and I'll be there!" I heard her, I know I did — It was her voice! And "What's the big deal?" was the furthest thing from my mind…"

Her son Marc, who flew to the crash site from California, later confirmed for them that Angie hadn't suffered; it had been over within seconds. Judie told me that, "…the message that I received from Angie has given Barrie and I much peace. We know that she was trying her best to assuage our pain. So many times our loved ones are communicating with us and we fail to recognize it. I say, look for every sign, small or big and don't let anyone negate what we know in our heart is true."

I couldn't have said it better myself.

15

Classic Symptom List

One of the benefits of having good grief partners is the ability to compare notes. Conversations with Barrie and Judie verified that I had done a good job capturing the correct items identified in my "Mourner's Guide". Our discussions also made me aware that unconsciously I had been making a list of classic symptoms, both physical and mental, that people experiencing loss seemed to have in common.

At the top of that list is **weight loss/weight gain**. Katie and I lost two dress sizes the first month after Ryan's death. We just couldn't seem to eat. When we found our appetites again, we couldn't stop eating. We gained the weight we'd lost back, and then some. We just accepted these changes and bought larger sizes until we felt better equipped to deal with it.

Grief can take your immune system down to nothing. **Sickness** became something we couldn't outrun. Colds, hives, back pain, chest pains, sleeplessness, fatigue; the list goes on and on. I couldn't get my hands to stop shaking and experienced occasional numbness in my arms and legs. At first, I thought the trembling was a reaction to the medicine I was taking. But, it was simply a by-product of all the stress. None of this is uncommon, but that doesn't mean you should ignore any of the symptoms you might exhibit. Always get anything out of the ordinary checked out by a physician.

The sudden **inability to concentrate and lack of memory** was frustrating. Day in and day out, I'd end up walking in circles due to my

forgetfulness. Sticky notes became my best friends and helped me to keep track of daily responsibilities. The lack of concentration was even more annoying. My mind was jumping all over the place and I had to constantly be reminded of where I'd been going or what I'd been saying in order to complete many tasks or conversations. The failure to recall memories of Ryan was the hardest part. My doctor said it was just my mind/body protecting me, but in this situation, it felt as if they had turned against me. When I started to relax a little, those memories gradually came back to me.

Overwhelming **guilt** and constant **mind traffic** are standard symptoms for anyone dealing with suicide, but they are *not limited* to suicide. All of the "could haves, should haves, and would haves" can drive a person crazy. Putting all guilt driven thoughts down on paper helps to control them, and then they can be addressed one at a time. That's where the mind traffic comes from. It is the inner voice working through guilt on a continuous loop. Sometimes the only way to stop that traffic is to focus on the *Serenity Prayer*. Whenever guilt threatens to take me under, I recite it:

The Serenity Prayer
God grant me the serenity
to accept the things I cannot change;
courage to change the things I can;
and wisdom to know the difference.
~Reinhold Niebuhr

Parental paranoia is a common problem, with no real solution except — "Let go and let God." I believe I fought against this anxiety almost as hard as I did against the grief. It is natural to be protective of our children, but it has to be within reason. We could not lock Katie up in her room. I wanted what was going to be best for her, and this meant going forward with as much normalcy as possible. I just kept remembering how closely we had watched over our son, and how in the end, he had shot himself at home. That proved how worthless worrying really was.

All of these things were obstacles to overcome, and I soon realized that grief was work and a full-time job for anyone that wanted to survive loss. I accepted that this was my fate, but vowed that it wouldn't last forever. I faced each obstacle one at a time and continued to push forward.

Build a Toolbox

There is value in writing things down, especially when you're struggling with the symptoms of grief. I decided to make a list of all the things we'd done that had seemed to help us, with the intention of sharing them with others. I call these things "tools."

✓ **Anti-depressants:** Talk with your physician about taking something to get you over the hump. There is no shame in it. I can guarantee that no one is going to give you a medal for toughing it out, so don't suffer needlessly. You're going to hurt no matter what you do, but these at least enable you to function.

✓ **Cry:** You don't always have to be stoic or strong. There will be a time and a place for strength. When you are sad and distraught find a quiet place and *let yourself cry*. It's natural and healing to react in this way — so let it out. This isn't authorization to do it all day, but it is permissible and beneficial to cry when you need to.

✓ **Remember them:** Instead of spending all your time trying not to think about your deceased loved ones, set aside time each day specifically to *remember them*. Find a place where you can sit uninterrupted and allow yourself to recall the

fond memories you shared. Fighting the inevitable serves
no purpose, so work *with* your feelings. Make this time
a positive and healing thing to look forward to — for as
long as you need it.

✓ **If you're tired, sleep:** The stress and shock our bodies go
through is incredible. Learn to listen to what your body is
saying to you. I don't care what your mother told you, taking a nap in the middle of the day is perfectly acceptable.
Trust me; everything is a little easier if you can get some
sleep, wherever and whenever you can.

✓ **Do what you can, when you can:** Your energy will come
in waves, so utilize it when you have it. Bursts of energy
are opportunities to do the things you can't seem to tackle
when you're on the low end of the roller coaster. Try to pri-
oritize your tasks and responsibilities, and then you will be
ready to take on a few when your vigor returns.

✓ **Proper diet and exercise:** No mystery here...The correct
foods will build up your immune system and improve
your mental and physical state. Exercise will help with
your depression, fatigue, and sleep issues. Use the buddy
system to stay motivated.

✓ **Minimize the use of alcoholic beverage:** Drowning your
sorrows in alcohol is an easy thing to do, but don't do it. It
will make your depression worse and it will stall any progress you might be making toward recovery.

✓ **Get out of the house:** When you feel yourself getting sucked into the black hole, get in the car and go somewhere. Better yet, pick up a friend and do something together. Being home alone too much can be unhealthy. At the very least, try to leave the confinements of the house and go outside; get a change of scenery and some fresh air. Recovery requires action — so move it.

✓ **Grief Counseling:** Talk therapy is probably the most important tool in your toolbox. Talking to a grief counselor will give you the opportunity to say what's on your mind without being judged. If you don't have health insurance for counseling, then contact a community grief group. There are also local chapters of national organizations (i.e. Compassionate Friends, Survivors of Suicide (SOS), and Parents of Suicide) that provide support to the bereaved. Select a group that deals with your specific situation (spouse/child, suicide/murder) and attend their meetings. The people who belong to these groups "get it" and nothing feels better than being able to share with people who truly understand.

✓ **Talk to your friends:** If you hesitate to talk about your personal life with strangers, or just aren't ready for a support group, then try talking to your friends. There are certain things we are only able to share with people who know and love us. Getting things out into the open air will improve your state of mind and general well being. It doesn't matter *how* you get talk therapy — it only matters that *you do.*

✓ **Write a letter to your loved one or keep a personal journal:** Writing my thoughts and feelings down in letters to Ryan was very helpful to me. Some people prefer to keep a personal journal, but it doesn't matter which one you utilize to document your emotions and experiences. Having this personal record allows you to go back and read what you've written later. In review, you'll see how far you have come in your recovery. Sometimes you feel as though you are standing still — this provides proof that you're not.

✓ **Allow yourself the right to laugh and enjoy yourself:** Venture out to social gatherings with your friends. You don't have to stay long if you don't feel up to it, but at least try. You'll benefit from being with people that care for you. My friend Lori invited us to everything. Once, after turning her down several times in a row, she patiently told me, "That's okay Sal, but I'm not going to stop asking." That's a great friend. Her comment motivated me to make more of an effort to get out, and in return, I felt much better.

✓ **Get a dog or pet of your choice:** There is nothing like unconditional love, and pets have that to offer all day, every day. Our dog Maxx is one of the best tools in our toolbox, and by far the most valuable one we own.

✓ **Make a scrapbook of your loved one:** This was Katie's first project; I recommend it highly to anyone grieving a loss. It was very therapeutic for her to go through all of our photo albums and put her favorite pictures into one book. This also made it convenient for reminiscing. When the overwhelming urge to see your loved one occurs, you can reach for this book and enjoy the treasure of memories inside.

✓ **Memory box:** I keep a box of Ryan's personal items in his room. I created this tool to keep my need for physical touch at bay. Inside the box, I put a few of the items I treasured most. This provides a contained source of comfort. When I feel the need to touch him, touching his things is what gets me over the hump.

✓ **Re-decorate:** Just about every grieving person I've met has used decorating as a tool. I rearranged our furniture, pictures, and accessories in the main living area. We painted the master bedroom a different color and completely renovated Katie's bedroom by painting, wallpapering and adding new linens. This did wonders for all of us mentally, and was worth the time and effort it took to physically create change.

✓ **Reach out to other grieving families:** One day you will be able to help someone else walk this path of grief, as others are doing for you now. It is both healing and rewarding to be able to share your story and experiences with people who are newly bereaved.

✓ **Read:** I read all kinds of books: spiritual, metaphysical, scientific, biographical, and self-help. Books helped to fill my mind with the promise of something better, instead of constantly dwelling on my sadness and guilt. If you're not

a reader, get some books on tape and listen to what these authors have to say.

✓ **Meditation:** Most everything I read stressed the importance and benefits of learning mediation. It makes sense to me now, but didn't when I first read it. Grief is something we carry with us day in and day out. Meditation can give your mind and body a break from that pain. When you practice awareness (being in the moment), you learn to experience only what is right here — right now. Ryan's death is something that happened in the past, but my thoughts are what bring it into the present and future. Part of recovery resides in the ability to control our thoughts, so we do not have to drag our pain into every minute of every day. Meditation is the tool that can help us to do that.

Tools have to be used to be helpful. It is hard to stay focused and always remember those things that can provide assistance. My advice is to keep your toolbox close, and utilize what it has to offer. It's either that, or suffer the consequences.

1 7

Miss Lori

My friend Lori and I met in high school. After graduation, we went our separate ways. Both of us moved out of state for a period of time, married, had children, and then ended up right back where we had started — in our hometown. Both of our families belonged to the local athletic club and because of this, our paths crossed once again.

Our renewed friendship was primarily social at the start, but the more time we spent together, the closer we became. I found myself confiding in Lori about the difficulties we were having with our son, and the problems I had uncovered at the high school that were contributing to the situation. We shared our concerns as parents often do, and tried to learn from one another.

As I mentioned previously, she and her husband came over to our house the evening of Ryan's death. I was in my office when they arrived. Lori walked in and softly spoke my name. I had been sitting in the dark with my back to the door, and so it startled me a little when she entered. I remember standing up and turning to look at her. Her face was wet with tears. I appreciated the honesty with which she displayed her emotions because it allowed me to open up and do the same. We held each other; her embrace felt so comforting, I didn't want to let go.

Lori shared that her husband had been concerned about their coming over, but she had insisted. That's how she is — kind, caring and confident. I reassured her that they had done the right thing and thanked her for listening to her heart. For some reason people thought we should be left alone. In some cases, this may be true, but we didn't feel that way. We welcomed those who came and were grateful for the support they so generously offered to us.

I had a close friend at the time of Ryan's death, but she didn't handle the suicide well and we soon parted ways. Lori stood by me and helped me through the longest and most difficult days of my life. I never would have expected that she would be the one to do this for me, but I am grateful and glad that it turned out the way it did. She became my confidante and the value her friendship has added to my life is immeasurable. Let me put it this way — if I had to write a check for all that she has given me — *I wouldn't be able to afford her.*

Lori kept me from spending that entire first summer in the black hole. Her down to earth approach and innate good humor are what helped to keep me grounded. She was my talk therapy. With her, I could discuss anything and everything. Topics that would make other people uncomfortable didn't faze her a bit, which was a good thing. There were a slew of random things running through my mind, and I could never really be sure of what was going to surface during our conversations.

My biggest concerns always seemed to lead back to my state of mind; I was afraid of going crazy. Talking with Lori helped to alleviate these fears and she was always ready and willing to give me a reality check when I needed one. The collective effort of everything she helped guide me through ensured my complete trust in her.

I shared my thoughts about Lori one day with Katie, soon after I had confided in her about one of Ryan's "miracles." I said, "Lori believes that what we are experiencing is real too. I trust her — so if she says I'm not crazy — then I'm not." Ryan must have heard me express my faith in her opinion, because shortly after that Lori began to get things from him too…

My very first Mother's Day would have been excruciatingly painful had it not been for my friend and her ability to remain "open." A week before the holiday, while standing at our mailbox, I said out loud to Ryan, "I wish you could think of a way to send me a Mother's Day card Buddy...It would mean so much to me." Silently I had been dreading that day, because Ryan had made me a mother. For that reason alone, Mother's Day would always be difficult. That frustrated me, because I didn't want to make it a sad day; there was Katie and her feelings to consider. I kept my request for a card to myself and settled on making a plan for the day, one that would keep emotional triggers at bay.

I received a card in the mail a few days before Mother's Day. I noticed from the return address that it was from Lori. I opened it and my eyes soon brimmed with tears as I read what she had written inside:

"Sal, I was thinking about you and Mother's Day. I imagined how hard this day could be for you with Ryan gone, *so I'm sending this card not only as a friend, but on behalf of Ryan.* I know Ryan would want you to be happy on Mother's Day, and every day. You're a great Mom Sal, both of your children love you, I've seen it in their eyes, I know this is true. So...on this day, please recognize, you're among the very best, you own this day, be good to yourself!
Love, Lori"

I called her as soon as I was able to collect myself. When I reached her on the phone, she told me it had been the strangest thing; she had felt this sudden urgency to buy a card for me. It had taken her some time to select it, because she wasn't sure what type of card to get, but settled on "from one friend to another" in honor of Mother's Day. She told me she felt as if she had been guided to do this for me.

I waited until she was finished, then I told her of the request I had made at the mailbox that day. We both knew, in that moment, that something rare and beautiful had taken place. Anyone else would have blown it off as a "crazy coincidence," but Lori embraced it with me. It was clear from the sound of her voice that she was excited to have been a part of something so magical. Ryan found a reliable messenger in Lori. This was the first of the many messages she would deliver for him in the years to come.

My favorite miracles are those I receive through others. I love them because they arrive totally unexpected, and they are automatically validated because someone else shares the experience with you. This provides a built in "witness," which is helpful when dealing with skepticism. Second parties provide proof that we aren't imagining these things or making something up to feign contact out of our longing for our loved one, as some people would lead you to believe. Ryan knows this, and often uses other people as messengers to strengthen the case for miracles and the fact that they do exist.

If you are emotionally distressed or preoccupied with your pain, it is sometimes difficult for spirits to get through. In those situations, using a courier is the only way for them to reach us. The funny thing about a couriered message is that the courier usually has no clue of why they are doing what they are doing. The realization doesn't really occur to them until they make contact with the receiver. It is in putting the two together that the miracle is acknowledged and revered.

I spent that Mother's Day with my beautiful daughter and was actually able to focus and enjoy it with her. I made the choice to consider myself lucky, despite my current set of circumstances. I had one child in heaven that had proven he was still capable of showing me his love, and another child on earth whose love I could physically see and embrace. Changing my way of thinking had made it possible for me to celebrate that day. This made me realize that in order to overcome the challenges death had forced upon me, I would have to work on how I processed my thoughts. It was an important lesson to learn, and thanks to Lori — the easiest one yet.

18

Music and Miracle Basics

HAVE YOU EVER HAD something you wanted to say to someone, but couldn't quite find the words, or way to say it? I believe that music has a universal quality that enables it to do this for us. It can corral human emotions, thoughts, and feelings in a way that is both moving and magical. Music is one of the rare things in life that has the ability to reach inside of us and touch our souls. Grieving people are very sensitive and notice the impact of music right away. When you are hurting, it is sometimes too painful to listen to, but when it is used to deliver a sign — it can be quite euphoric.

Ryan was always a smart kid and that didn't change when he "crossed over". Ever observant, he clearly noted the effect music was having on us. Radios operate on electrical energy and this made it very easy for him to manipulate (just as he did earlier with the microwave and TV). Ryan took advantage of this and used it to get our attention, answer our questions, or just to validate he was near.

I mentioned earlier that my brother David wrote and delivered Ryan's eulogy. In his closing, David had surprised us all by singing "The Dance" by Garth Brooks — a cappella. There wasn't a dry eye in the room when he finished. It was so beautiful. Because of this event, "The Dance" became the number one song we associated with Ryan. He picked up on that fact, and always uses it as his heavy hitter. As obtuse as we can sometimes be, we never fail to pick up on this one because it's right on our radar.

The Reason

I remember the first time Ryan used it on me. It happened early one morning on my way to work. I was sitting in the car and had paused at the end of our driveway. I was already having a tough day. I closed my eyes and said "Ryan, I miss you so much — tell me, are you here with me now?" The radio went into dead silence, then "The Dance" began to play. I could hardly believe my ears. *I could feel him*, and so I reached my hand over to the passenger seat and rested it there as I listened to the song play. After that, there was no doubt in my mind that he was using music to communicate with us.

Ryan did love country music, but that wasn't the only type he enjoyed. In his late teens he also developed a love for some classic 70's and 80's tunes. Katie made a CD so a few of his favorites could be played at the funeral service. They were "Sweet Home Alabama" (Lynyrd Skynyrd), "Life's Been Good" (Joe Walsh), and "Devil Went Down to Georgia" (Charlie Daniels). These also became a part of Ryan's playlist for us.

We all have our own special songs. Joe usually gets "The Dance" or "One More Day" (Diamond Rio). I often get "Sweet Home Alabama," but my special Momma songs are "One More Day," "I Need You" (LeAnn Rimes), "Drops of Jupiter" (Train), "Calling All Angels" (Train), or "You'll be in my Heart" by Phil Collins. The music varies depending on the circumstance or person. I know that as each year passes my playlist changes, because I do.

One of my favorite musical miracles happened on my way to pick up Maxx from the groomer. I had spent 20 minutes of "Ryan time" in the window seat at home before leaving the house. Devoting a block of time to my grieving each morning helped me to get through the rest of the day. I had ended my time by saying, "I hope you are listening to me Ryan and know how very much I love you. Can you see me? I wish that I knew…Just give me a little sign if you can. Please watch over us Cowboy (his nickname)."

I was in the car and about a block from home when the sun visor on the driver's side snapped, as if someone had reached down and tweaked it. This startled me and got my attention. I reached my hand up to touch the photo of Ryan I always keep there. Right then "Every Breath You Take" by Sting started to play on the radio. As I listened to the lyrics, I realized Ryan had provided the perfect way to answer my earlier request of "Can you see me?" In my book, *signs don't come much clearer than that.*

Another musical favorite included my daughter. One afternoon Katie and I decided to get a pedicure together. We went to the local day spa where Ryan had once purchased the "Executive Spa Package" for me as a gift for Mother's Day. My husband had purchased the "Standard Spa Package" for me that same year. Joe had taken a lot of teasing over the fact that Ryan had trumped him on his package selection for me by choosing the "Executive" over the "Standard."

We were laughing about this when all of the sudden "One More Day" came on the radio. Katie reached for my hand and pointed to the speaker on the wall. "Listen," she said. We sat in amazement listening as the song played out. This was Ryan's way of letting us know that he was there, remembering with us and sharing in our laughter. Katie picked up on that, and it made me happy to know she was alert and open to the messages he was sending.

I am in awe of the many gifts this kind of communication offers. I especially like the fact that it is nothing we can possibly control. You cannot simply will a song to come on the radio. I have spoken to other grieving families/individuals and have found that this type of spirit contact is something many of us share. "Only the Good Die Young" (Billy Joel), "The Reason" (Hoobastank), and "Go Rest High On that Mountain" (Vince Gill), are songs that parents of suicide seem to have in common. The significance of hearing the musical miracles of others is that it validated the experience for us and confirmed our gut instincts.

The Reason

I came to several very important conclusions as the end of year one crept closer. The first was that Ryan was totally in charge when it came to delivering the things we describe as signs and miracles. If I'd had any say in the matter, I would be getting them all day, every day, but this is not the case. You can ask until the cows come home, but one thing is certain: *those things will never come when you are looking for them.* That would defeat their purpose. We get them when we need them most, and spirits decide *when* and *how* they are sent. If we could order them on demand, they would lose their significance.

Secondly, whoever said, "timing is everything" was correct. When I looked back, I also realized it wasn't so much *how* (through someone else or by ourselves) or *what* (music, telephone or TV) we got, it was *when* the signs were delivered that gave them importance. *The TIMING makes the miracle.*

The sole purpose of any sign is to heal us, by giving us hope. The source of our grief stems from the pain of being separated from our loved ones. These points of contact are to reassure us that their spirits are still here with us, and knowing this makes each passing day more bearable. If you allow yourself to believe, you will begin to take comfort in the things they provide, and the intensity of your grief will begin to lessen.

These facts provided several pieces to the puzzle that Ryan's death had presented to us. I put them in place and stepped back to review all that I had learned. Slowly but surely, I could see our path to recovery was beginning to unfold. Most of what I had learned so far had come from the ability to trust my gut instincts. Knowing this, I made the decision to give my intuition a free rein and trusted that it would continue to pull us in the right direction. As it turns out, I bet on the right horse — because that's exactly what it did.

19

DIAMOND RIO

WE DID PRETTY WELL at the one year mark. No one had to work because Ryan's death date fell on a Saturday that year. A few people stopped by the house, and many others either called or sent a card. The days leading up to Ryan's death date seemed harder than the actual day itself. I suppose it was just remembering the events that led up to his suicide that pulled us down that week before. We had focused on getting through the first year, and now that we had, we weren't sure of what our next steps would be.

There wasn't much time to think about it, because just two weeks later we celebrated what would have been his 21st birthday. Ryan's death date and birthday are so close together that it doesn't give anyone much time to recover in between. He died just before his 20th birthday, so we had already hit this milestone once. I attempted to make it a happy day, but regardless of my efforts, his birthday proved to be very difficult for me. I had to allow myself several wallowing periods in order to get through it.

That afternoon I purchased four helium birthday balloons. I delivered the first one to the cemetery. While there, I pulled out one of those mini-bottles of Jack Daniels (Ryan's favorite) and drank a toast to my son. I spent some time alone with him there and recalled a few of our favorite birthdays together. I'd given him a big surprise party to celebrate his 18th and my thoughts turned to that day, and how grateful I was to have done that for him.

The Reason

At home, we all wrote a special message to Ryan and tied them to the streamers on each of the three remaining balloons. Joe, Katie and I gathered out on the deck. I had saved a big firework from the fourth of July, and Joe lit this like a birthday candle. We all released our individual balloons into the atmosphere as we sang "Happy Birthday" to him. This has become our family tradition and each year we commemorate Ryan's birthday in this way.

A week after his birthday we loaded into the car to go to a Diamond Rio concert. Katie had signed all three of us up for their fan club a few months earlier. You had to be members of the fan club before you could sign up for "meet and greet" privileges held before the concert. Katie had all the details down ahead of time and our names were on the list to meet the band. Knowing this, I had grabbed one of Ryan's senior pictures and had written his name on the back of it. It was our plan to ask them to dedicate one of our favorite songs to Ryan at this performance.

We had been talking about it all week and joked with my parents that they were going to miss it if they didn't come. Mom and Dad managed to get concert tickets at the last minute, and we saw them in the bleachers when we arrived at the amphitheater. As it turned out there were a lot of people in the audience that night that we knew. Sinbad's wife (Joe's friend that had passed) was there, several of my husband's cousins, and our seats were next to a few women I knew from our hometown. Everything felt just right, and I prayed that our reason for being there would come to fruition.

Shortly after our arrival, they called for the "meet and greet" group and we got into the line to go backstage. All the band members were very polite and friendly, posing for pictures with all of their fans. I spotted their lead singer, Marty, and headed straight for him. Katie and I had our pictures taken with him and then I handed him Ryan's picture. I told him that I had lost my son a year ago and that they were one of his favorite bands. I explained to Marty how much it would mean to my family if they would dedicate one of their songs to him at the concert that night. I told him that "One More Day" and "I Believe" were two of our favorites.

Marty gave me a warm hug, but said that he couldn't promise anything. He explained that ever since 9/11 everyone wanted those songs dedicated to their deceased loved ones. I told him I understood, but reiterated that if there were any way, it would mean the world to me. I pressed Ryan's picture into his hand, and turned to leave. Something made me look back a few seconds later, and when I did, our eyes met. I felt that was a good sign and I said a silent prayer that our request would be honored. Katie and I had our pictures taken with the other band members and then went back to our seats to wait for the concert to begin.

Joe had skipped the "meet and greet," but we filled him in on the details. It was a beautiful summer night and Diamond Rio played a wonderful concert. We sat through the entire show, waiting for Ryan's dedication. They played their last song, and then left the stage. Everyone kept clapping and soon they returned for their encore.

Marty started talking about the song "One More Day" and the impact it'd had on so many people. He told the audience that it had gotten a lot of air play due to Dale Earnhardt's passing and 9/11. Then he said, "I talked to a lady tonight backstage that recently lost her son, and she asked if I could dedicate a song to him. His name is Ryan Wecker and this song is for him and his family." With that, the band started to play "One More Day." It was one of the most beautiful moments of my life, and I will never forget it.

Something changed in all of us that night. I'm not sure what it was, but it was healing. It had just felt so good for us to be able to do something special for Ryan. It really brought closure to the whole damn year. I still marvel at the fact that we were actually able to pull it off and feel grateful that there are some entertainers out there with bigger hearts than egos. Diamond Rio's act of compassion renewed our faith in mankind and it provided us with a much needed boost as we headed into *year two…*

Me and Katie with Marty Roe,
the lead singer for the band "Diamond Rio"

2 0

THE PICTURES

THAT FALL WE TOOK Katie to college for her freshman year. She had chosen SVSU (Saginaw Valley State University) because she liked the smaller campus. I was thrilled because it was only 30 minutes from home and if we needed each other, it would be a quick trip. Katie received a scholarship, and was very excited about living on campus in the dorms with the other honor students.

I was secretly dreading the "empty nest." I didn't know how I was going to be on my own. Katie had become my constant companion and I knew that not having her around on a daily basis was going to be a very difficult adjustment for me. I kept these concerns to myself and tried to show enthusiasm as we planned for her college departure.

It had been a difficult summer for Katie and I was counting on the change in environment to help her move forward. At SVSU she wouldn't be "the sister who's brother had shot himself" like she'd been her senior year at the high school. This was a fresh start for her; anonymity being the most important part of what her new beginning had to offer. She had secured a part-time job near school, so with that and a full class schedule, we hoped she'd be busy enough to stay out of trouble.

I believe most parents of a college freshman worry about the partying and the potential problems associated with being away from home for the first time — we were no different. My main concern was the anger she still harbored and the difficulty she had expressing her grief. I had tried to get her back into counseling, but Katie told me that until we could find someone that "got it" she wasn't going down that road again…She reassured me that she'd be fine and I had no choice but to believe her.

Joe and I drove her up to the SVSU campus and helped her settle into her new dorm room. While unloading our van we discovered that Sinbad's daughter and her cousin were going to be staying in the same building. Joe helped them move some of their things in too. I was quite sure that meeting up with them had been *no coincidence*. Over the years, Sinbad had called on my husband several times to give his family a hand when he was out of town. His death had not stopped him from arranging for Joe to help once more.

We hung around until Katie finally pushed us out the door. I hugged her goodbye and smiled, then sobbed during the entire drive home. The house felt so quiet and empty without her. I wandered from room to room and eventually into both Ryan and Katie's bedrooms. Staring at their vacant havens reawakened my grief and it wasn't long before I found myself engulfed by the black hole.

In the days that followed I could feel old wounds were reopening. I forced myself to accept my current set of circumstances and focused my attention on adjusting to them, instead of dwelling on my loneliness. I learned to pacify my need for physical closeness with the telephone conversations Katie and I had several times a day. This and e-mail helped to ease the transition some. She came home for occasional weekends and I looked forward to longer visits with her during the holidays. Ever sensitive to my needs, Katie was generous with her time and devoted a large chunk to me as I regrouped.

My bigger problem was thinking too much. I was fine at work, but there was a large chunk of time between Joe's arrival and me getting home. I tried to compensate by staying later at the office, and then would run errands on the way home. This filled some of the gaps but it wasn't enough to keep me from dwelling on the suicide, something I had started to do again — in excess.

I was still quite preoccupied with that day, primarily because I hadn't been there to experience the course of events as they had unfolded. There was a void between my leaving for work and arriving home after the fact. I had managed to put a few things together by gathering information from the others, but it had been such a traumatic time; most everyone's account was sketchy at best. My imagination ran wild trying to account for the lost time in between my experience and what they'd been able to share with me.

My quest for answers is what sent me in pursuit of the photos the police had taken. I became convinced that I would find what I was looking for in them. I believed that as a mother, my trained eye would be capable of seeing any details that had been overlooked, and that they would provide the closure I so desperately needed.

I had already requested to see the photos several times. Every time I'd get up the nerve to go down to the police department and ask, they would refuse to show them to me. When I approached them this time, they said I would have to process an F.O.I.A. (Freedom of Information Act) request in order to get access to them.

I was given this information as I stood at the counter in the police department. From where I was standing, I could see the reflection of the officer who had denied my request in the glass of a picture hanging on the wall. He'd argued with me and then had walked around the corner, unaware that I was still able to see him. I watched as he extracted Ryan's file folder from the filing cabinet, pulling the photos from inside. He stood there and flipped through them, one by one.

I continued to stare at his reflection, even as I pleaded my case to the woman behind the counter (who had been left to deal with me). It angered and infuriated me to be denied my request for the pictures, when just around the corner that officer freely shuffled through them. I went to my attorney the next day and had him process the F.O.I.A. request.

I'm sure it will be hard for people to fully comprehend my need to see these photos. I'm certain that my explanation will seem inadequate to many inquisitive minds. But the truth is, I don't really need to justify my request to anyone — it was just something I felt I had to do.

My attorney processed the necessary paperwork. He called a few days later to tell me that the photos were ready to be picked up at his office. When I went to the office to get them, I was asked to please make sure someone else would be home with me before I viewed them. I was also handed a letter that the F.O.I.A. officer had written to me. In return, I gave them a copy of a poem I had written; inspired by my struggle to obtain what I felt was rightfully mine...

There is Something You Should Know
When You Address a Mother Who Has Lost Her Child

She has already suffered the worst pain
she will ever have to endure...
The love and protective nature she inherited upon the
birth of her child will live inside her — FOREVER.
Death does not end the bond that birth established.

Though she may look hardened to the naked eye —
she is a well of softness.
The hardness is just a shell to protect her wounded soul.

To touch her child's skin — be it clean or covered in blood,
Is still the most comforting action she can take...
Don't take that from her.

Don't imagine her reaction — she is doing
what is instinctual and natural…

It hurts no one and she will live with that memory
until her last breath.
It is closure.
This is the only comfort she will know in the endless sea
of misery that she has been thrust into…

Death is the separation of physical touch — allow her this last
point of contact in her darkest hour.

Knowledge is the key for going forward.
It is her armor against the tests of grief that time will impose.
It is important to have the facts straight — allowing little
room for an already overactive imagination. She needs to
know their final moments — just as she witnessed their
first breath.

Unless you have lost a child — *You will never know what she*
knows and will never be able to understand.…
So be grateful, gracious, kind, and respectful
of the fact that —
You stand outside the garden of grief *that she will be tending*
for the rest of her life.

As with everything else in this world we live in — death
is an experience to learn from.
Grieving Mothers are your source of knowledge —
So quiet the voice inside of you, and listen to what THEY are
saying…

~S.E.G 2003

When I got home, I put all of my belongings on the kitchen table and then went outside to have a smoke. Now that I had the pictures — I wasn't so sure of what I wanted to do with them. I was alone in the house and this gave me time to think. It was a clear October night and the sky was filled with stars. I felt so overwhelmed by the decision at hand that I sat down on the deck and lowered my head into folded arms. I found myself crying as I mentally wrestled with my choices. More than anything I wanted someone to tell me what to do, however, I knew that no one could — except maybe God.

It wasn't my nature at the time to succumb to prayer. In fact, before Ryan died, I prayed very little. The truth was I hadn't believed it would do any good. But like everything else, my views and understanding were changing, and so I got on my knees and begged for help.

I don't pray like other people. I just talk, like I'm talking to a friend. Doing it this way feels more genuine to me, less ceremonial and un-hypocritical. I suppose I just have a different way of looking at things. I believe that it isn't important how a person prays — as long as it is genuine and gets the job done.

I remember exactly what I prayed for, and I spoke each syllable with heartfelt passion. "God please help me — I don't know what to do. Everyone says I shouldn't look at the pictures, but I feel a need to know what happened that day. I just love my son so much. I'm so lost without him. If I knew that Ryan loved me — if there was a way for him to tell me that he loved me — I would seal that envelope shut and put those pictures away. I need a sign, and I need it badly. *Please help me, please, please…*"

After my plea for help, I had a good, hard cry. It was the kind of crying that leaves you breathless, and the lack of oxygen makes you want to throw up. I let it all out and when I was done, I felt exhausted, but better. There was nothing more that I could do. Maxx sat next to me and tried to give me comfort. I welcomed his efforts and shortly thereafter, we went inside to get some tissues.

I wandered back into the kitchen and started to pick up the mess I'd left on the table. I set the photos aside for the time being, but decided it would be all right to read the letter that the F.O.I.A. officer had written.

In his letter, he introduced himself and shared that he had knowledge of a similar experience. He stated that because of it, he and his wife could probably identify with me better than most, but would be the first to say they could only imagine what I was feeling. He wrote "...what you are feeling is unique. Feelings are neither right nor wrong; they just are...Mainly, I wish to convey to you my humble but heartfelt opinion that you are good, your feelings are understandable, *your son loved you...*" I stopped right there.

"Your son loved you"...wasn't that exactly what I had prayed for? Hadn't I just 5 minutes ago asked God "...*If I knew that Ryan loved me — if there was a way for him to tell me that he loved me...*" I felt a hot rush go throughout my body, and then I began to tingle all over. Was this a sign? How could it be? My initial reaction was that my prayers had been answered, but the skeptic in me was asking the question, so I took a deep breath and re-read the letter. Every time I got to that sentence, the warm rush and the tingling started up. I closed my eyes and allowed myself to gracefully accept the help I'd been given. "Thank you," I whispered as I pulled the letter close to me...

I let out a sigh of relief, then took the envelope holding the pictures, and put them — unviewed — at the top of my bedroom closet. Hey, you don't mess with God. Although I still questioned whether it had *truly* been a sign, I decided that until I got another one, that's where the pictures were going to stay. Having resolved the issue of the pictures for now, I returned to the kitchen and finished reading the rest of his letter.

He went on to say "...Because suicide is so mystifying, people (even friends and family) do not know how to respond or what to do — so often they do nothing and slowly drift away…" He graciously offered that both he and his wife were ready to assist in any capacity they could. It appeared that his wife was a family therapist in a private practice and he made it clear that telling me this was not a solicitation, just a recommendation that professional counseling helps in this type of situation. "I hope you take this letter as intended — a sincere attempt to connect and show we care."

For the first time since Ryan's death, this gave me the chance to listen to someone that had actually dealt with a suicide (attempt) within his or her family. Everything he had said about their experience were things we had also found to be true. It was a godsend to know that his wife was also a licensed therapist. This made her a professional that "got it." Because of this, I felt sure that she would be someone Katie could open up to. It was a second prayer answered.

Because his letter had been so heartfelt and honest, I was compelled to reply in kind. This gave me something to do while I waited for Joe to come home. Later, during dinner, I recanted to my husband the latest miracle I'd received. Even as I told him my story, I felt that nagging doubt, so while sitting at the table I asked for a second sign, just to confirm I'd gotten the first one right.

Two days later I received a card in the mail with no return address on the envelope. Inside the card on a separate piece of paper was a poem entitled "God's Garden." The card itself was religious in nature and the sender had taken the time to write a lengthy note to me. It was signed by a woman named Carla, and it had a post script that she was the person who had recently done my mammogram. Inside she wrote:

> "Sally, Just a note to let you know you are in my thoughts and prayers. It was a pleasure to have met you. You are very strong. Just remember to keep faith in God and (that) he is

always there beside you along with your son. They are walking hand in hand and *they love you very much...*"

You could have literally knocked me over with a feather. What are the chances that a complete stranger would send me a card two days after I'd asked for another sign? Let alone a sign that clearly stated *I was loved*. My second sign had been delivered. I don't care if you call me crazy all day long. Some things you just know, and this was one of them.

2 1

I Get My Hug

It was a mystery to me how all of those events had come together so effortlessly, putting everything neatly in its place. Perhaps this was how things were suppose to be, instead of clawing and fighting for every little step we took forward. I couldn't shake the feeling that I was missing something very important — something that would make our journey through grief much easier. Two months later, I figured it out.

In December of 2003, my younger sister Stephanie called to remind us of the "Worldwide Candle Lighting" held by The Compassionate Friends. This event is held on the 2nd Sunday in December. It "…unites family and friends around the globe as they light candles for one hour to honor and remember children who have died at any age, from any cause. As candles are lit at 7 p.m. local time, creating a virtual wave of light, hundreds of thousands of persons commemorate and honor the memories of children in a way that transcends all ethnic, cultural, religious, and political boundaries."

It was our first time to participate in this annual event. I lit a candle for Ryan and one for Angie, Barrie and Judie's daughter too. I sat in silence for awhile, watching the dancing flames of the candles before going outside on the deck to have my evening chat with God and Ryan. It had become a ritual to communicate with them in this way; I feel close to them there. That night along with my thanks, I made a special request for Christmas. I asked for a visit from Ryan. I mentioned that I was still waiting for my hug and that it would make a great present for me if he felt ready to give me one.

I didn't have to wait for Christmas. That night, in the middle of a dream — kind of like a commercial break — Ryan appeared. He was surrounded by a sea of whiteness; I saw him standing there in a white t-shirt and blue jeans. I called out his name as I ran toward to him. I took him into my arms and said, "Oh Ryan, you feel so good." I pulled my son close, pressing every inch of myself tightly against him.

My senses drank him in. I could see him, smell him, and feel him. There are no words in the English language to describe that embrace with justice. I felt complete peace and love in such volumes that it filled every pore in my body. Our love formed a river, and I could feel it flowing from my heart into his as I held him. It was a blending of souls, which formed a single, unbreakable bond. The intensity of that moment was so powerful and pure; it was unlike anything I have ever experienced. It was *heaven*...

Ryan spoke to me and said, "You feel so damn good too, Momma." Hearing his voice was as sweet as eating chocolate for breakfast, and I indulged heartily. Pulling back, I gazed into his beautiful, blue eyes. Then I called to Katie, because I wanted her to see him too, but when I turned around to look for her, Ryan disappeared. Commercial over! Right away, my other dream picked up, right where it had left off.

When I awoke my memory of our hug was crystal clear. It is important to note that there is a distinct difference between *dreams* of our loved ones and *visits* from them. The clarity with which we can recall their visits and the details they provide, help to distinguish them from our regular dreams. Also, the overall experience of a visit is completely different from that of a dream — they just feel *more real*.

I basked in the memory of Ryan's visit. At long last, I had received the hug promised to me in the very first reading I'd had with Elaine. I replayed it over, and over again in my mind — which is how I figured out that missing "something" I had been looking for...

I had *asked* for help, and my request had been entirely *heartfelt.* Reviewing my miraculous experiences helped me to see these common denominators. Identifying them also reminded me of something I had recently read in one of my spiritual magazines; I looked for and located the article in question. Smiling, I read the text that I had previously highlighted. It said, "Keep asking, and it will be given to you. Keep searching, and you will find. Keep knocking and the door will be opened for you." (Matthew 7:7)

Could it really be that easy? I contemplated this question at length and finally concluded that maybe it wasn't meant to be hard. Maybe the simplicity of the actions required are what made it difficult to grasp; we always make everything harder than it has to be. How often had I seen people refuse to ask for help, because they let their egos get in the way? A huge "Ah ha" washed over me; instinctively, I knew I had my answer. Common sense reminded me that using this formula successfully is what had identified it in the first place.

Part of recovery lies in the ability to get help when you need it most. Now I knew all I had to do was ask (in a form of prayer) — with heartfelt sincerity — to achieve this. Everything I had learned up to this point, however helpful, paled in comparison to this revelation. I still had much to learn, but fortunately, my quest to understand Ryan's death had led me into a virtual classroom, where I was learning the lessons designed to move me forward, not only through my grief, but also toward a deeper spiritual awareness. However challenging, the rewards for completing these lessons was turning out to be well worth the effort it took to learn them.

This lesson had caused me to see the purpose in my growing spirituality and the effect this awareness was having on my everyday life. Now I knew that Ryan wasn't alone in his efforts to help me, something

much greater than the two of us was most definitely working behind the scenes. My instructions were clear; I must "keep searching," and be willing to trust in the fact that my prayers for help were being received and would be answered. It appeared that Ryan's visit had delivered much more than a hug; I now held the *map out of hell* firmly in my grasp.

22

LEARNING CURVE

RYAN'S VISIT HAD BEEN perfectly timed because the lift it provided helped get me through the holidays; however, my depression increased as the winter dragged on. The weight I had gained over Christmas, paired with numerous health issues helped to deepen my despair. It was time for another diversion, and I decided that a warm weather vacation was something we could all benefit from. Due to Katie's college schedule, I planned our trip to coincide with her spring break. We chose Puerto Vallarta as our destination and I busied myself with trip preparations as the snow persistently fell.

I continued to work at my grief diligently. We had Barrie and Judie to share things with, so it was a bit easier now. Every lesson we learned helped them, and we shared our knowledge freely — as did they. I continued to educate myself through books, but also started to learn quite a bit about spirit contact by watching John Edward on TV.

I like him; John Edward has a down to earth approach and treats a grieving person with respect. At the end of each show, he always makes it a point to say that people don't need him to communicate with their deceased loved ones, that it is something we can do for ourselves. He emphasizes the importance of staying open and paying attention to the little things that occur in our daily lives.

Watching his program gave me the opportunity to see that many other normal, everyday people were as curious as I was about the afterlife. It also proved that grieving individuals often gravitate to readings with mediums to reassure them that their loved ones are all right, and to gain the information that validates this fact for them. This was a huge relief, because it took a lot of the "crazy" out of it for me.

I had also noticed that there were quite a few movies, songs, and television shows that reflected the phenomenon of spirit contact as well. It hadn't been that way when I was growing up. Most everything at that time regarding the possibilities of life after death was still discussed behind closed doors; it wasn't anything anyone shared publicly and certainly not on TV. I find it refreshing and helpful to see that now these topics are being addressed in public forums.

People began sharing their "miracles" with me soon after they discovered that I believed in the afterlife and had experienced spirit contact as well. I became someone they could share these things with without being thought of or treated as a "nut case." As a result, I felt less like a freak and more comfortable in the new world that was developing around me.

Ryan was learning in his new world too, and practiced a few new methods of contact on me that winter. In February of 2004, I had two unique incidents occur. One happened on Valentine's Day. I had sobbed like a baby after reading the card I had purchased for him aloud at the cemetery. Afterward, I mentioned that it would be comforting to get a sign from him to acknowledge that he had heard me. I made my way home and then decided that doing some laundry would help distract me from my sadness.

I had put a load in the washer, and was climbing the basement stairs when I stopped to look at a picture of Ryan that hung in the stairwell. All of the sudden I felt a good, strong, thump on the head! I stood perfectly still then looked up to see if a ceiling tile or something had fallen on my head, but nothing was there. I had to laugh! It had surprised me, but I knew what it was as soon as I stopped to think about it. I guess it was payback for all the "thumps" I had given him in the past, followed by "Hello, is anybody home?" I know he got a kick out of delivering that one!

The second incident happened shortly after that, while driving. It had been cold and cloudy for a week. Later that afternoon the sky cleared and the sun came out. I was on my way to the nail salon after work, and as I drove I was thinking, "What a nice day — I feel so much better when it's sunny out." Suddenly, out of nowhere, a voice said to me, "Yes, but you have to be careful on sunny days too!"

Whoa!!! Where did that come from? The hair stood up on the back of my neck. It spooked me, and I found myself exercising extra caution as I pulled up to an intersection seconds later. When the traffic light turned green, I turned right. A split second later, a girl driving a red car flew out of the parking lot to my right, straight into the street without stopping to look either way. I slammed on my brakes and just missed hitting her by a thread. I surely would have hit her had I not been cautioned earlier. The forewarning had heightened my sense of awareness and that had slowed me down which saved me and the other car from colliding. I was pretty shaken up, but more by the voice, than the close call with the red vehicle.

This is a good time to point out again, that we don't get to chose when or how we get our points of contact. It is equally important to note that you *don't always get what you want*, but *you will get what you need*. I've learned to go with the flow, and always make it a point to be grateful and say thank you whenever assistance is given.

Here is something to think about: Everything is energy — everything. Every person, tree, and bug, *even our thoughts are energy*. Albert Einstein taught us that $(E=mc^2)$. It is a fact of quantum physics that energy cannot be created, nor can it be destroyed. It can only be converted from one state or form to another. So, when our loved ones die, they simply shed their physical bodies; their energy remains unchanged. Because of this their spirits/souls continue to thrive — the difference is

that there is no mass in which they are contained. When you can wrap your mind around that, you'll find it easier to accept and believe in the little miracles we experience each and every day.

Opening the door to understanding takes both work and time. It took many more miracles before I was able to embrace and understand this theory. The crux of this is that anytime you entertain ideas that thrive out of the mainstream, you open yourself up for criticism. This part of my education took the longest to embrace simply due to that fact. In my weakened state of grief, I sometimes allowed the negative opinions of others to stifle my progress. Truth is, healing from grief is often an extremely slow process, so this gave me plenty of time to work through my ambivalence. I exercised my need for truth by continuing to observe and learn — one lesson at a time.

23

THE RING

I WAS GLAD WHEN it was finally March and the countdown to vacation was over. We arrived in Puerto Vallarta, Mexico to sunny skies, and it was a relief to find that the timeshare I had rented for us was as beautiful as advertised. We changed into our swimming suits and were soon sipping on cocktails and lounging on chaises that provided a magnificent ocean view. It was time to relax and enjoy the sunshine.

Katie had brought along a friend and they wandered off to check out the resort. My husband's pleasant nature soon had him making friends at the pool, and these new acquaintances provided us with great tips on where to golf, shop and dine. A restaurant named Pipi's came highly recommended, and after a few days of sun and relaxation, we decided to go into town and try it out.

Pipi's is famous for their jumbo margaritas and mariachi band. The atmosphere is lively and we enjoyed all it had to offer. I couldn't remember the last time we'd had this much fun and it felt wonderful. During dinner, I raised my margarita and made a toast. I said, "Ryan, I don't know if you can see us now, but if you can — I'll bet you are wishing you were here!" We all toasted him and then enjoyed our delicious meal.

Back at the resort, we took a little walk as we made our way back to the room. We were all joking and laughing when Katie said, "Shhhh, listen." From high up on one of the balconies, "Life's Been Good" played loudly on someone's radio. This was one of the songs from Ryan's funeral; it came straight from his playlist. Now, what are the chances that song would be playing as we walked across the resort to our room? After all, this was 2004 and that song came out in 1978. We were in Mexico and not the United States. Clearly, this was a sign from Ryan. He wanted us to know he wasn't missing a thing!

Later that week, we went back into town. Our vacation was almost over and we wanted to pick out a few souvenirs to take home. The girls had no problem finding several things to purchase, but I wasn't seeing anything that interested me. I followed Katie into a little shop that was filled with silver jewelry. I was aimlessly wandering around, when a display of rings suddenly captured my interest. One ring in particular caught my eye.

The design of the ring was very simple. It had a crescent moon on the right side, and a single star on the left. I picked it up and slipped it on. The moon and the star did not connect, but faced one another, giving the appearance that they were floating on my finger. I showed the ring to Katie and we both agreed that it was perfect. Joe purchased it for me as a gift, and I wore my ring for the rest of our vacation.

I began calling my new ring "Ryan's ring" and decided to wear it in memory of him. Originally, I had planned to purchase a locket to hold some clippings I had of Ryan's hair. My intention was to wear it as a piece of memorial jewelry, but I was unable to find a locket that I liked. The ring felt like a good alternative, so I changed my original plan to accommodate my need to wear something in his honor.

My ring seems to attract a lot of attention. Strangers are always noticing it and this often opens the door for conversation. I mention that I wear the ring in memory of my son, and 9 times out of 10, this prompts the person admiring it to share a story of their lost loved one. I appreciate these conversations because they provide an important opportunity for both parties to share something special. It is always a positive experience when it happens, and I feel that these moments make my ring unique in more ways than one.

A few weeks after our return from vacation, I stumbled across the notes I had taken during my second reading with Elaine and took the time to review them. As I read through the notes, I discovered a reference she had made regarding a "special ring"; I did not have one at the time of the reading. Intuitively, I knew now that "Ryan's ring" was the one she'd referred to. In readings, it isn't always clear where the information is coming from in regards to the future, present or past. In this circumstance, it had been a glimpse into my future. I no longer considered this reference a loose puzzle piece. Once identified, it went firmly into place.

Reading those notes inspired me, and I considered booking another appointment with Elaine; however, that idea never materialized into anything. Later that week I received an invitation in the mail to attend an event at a friend's home. This occasion provided the opportunity to sit with another medium. Her name was Nanci — and she was a channeler.

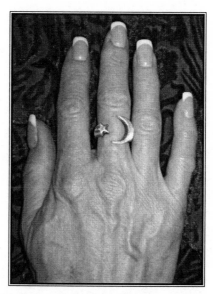

"Ryan's Ring" purchased in Puerto Vallarta

24

THE CHANNELER

I RECEIVED THE PREVIOUSLY mentioned invitation from my friend, Melanie, in March of 2004. Her social gathering was designed to offer purses, manicures, cosmetics and various other goods and services that women love to indulge in. Inside the invitation was a complete list of what would be available at the event.

I noticed right away that one of the services being offered were readings with "Nanci" — a psychic, channel, medium. I'd had such good luck with Elaine that I rarely saw anyone else, but I decided to test the waters and see what a complete stranger would have to say to me. All services needed to be booked prior to the party, so I called Melanie and made an appointment for my reading.

I had two weeks before the party and I spent that time thinking of what I wanted to ask Ryan. I thought of two things. One — I wanted him to tell me that he was sorry for the suicide. As a mother, I guess I saw it as a part of my job to ask for an apology. Two — I wanted him to clarify that he was the one I kept hearing in my mind. This was to reassure me that I wasn't losing my marbles. I was still a little shaken up from the warning I'd received the month before while out driving.

I found myself prepping Ryan for the impending reading. I told him when and where it would be and I repeated the two things I wanted to know several times — simply and specifically. I coached him at the cemetery and I spoke to him through the mirror in his bedroom. Lately I had found myself talking to him that way, mainly because I sensed his

presence when I did. It didn't feel strange or foolish to reach out to him in this way — just instinctual.

On the day of the party, I arrived at Melanie's a little early, which gave me time to mingle with several of the other guests. It wasn't long before my name was called and I was led upstairs to one of the bedrooms being used for the readings. Nanci greeted me warmly as I entered the room. Prior to the meeting I had been told to bring pictures of anyone I wanted information about. I handed her the three photos I'd brought with me of Joe, Ryan and Katie and then took a seat as I waited for the reading to begin.

The first thing she talked about didn't have anything to do with the pictures. Instead, she opened our reading by discussing my first marriage and former husband. For some reason she had picked up on these details from my past. Nanci gave a very clear description of both my ex-husband and the turbulent marriage we had shared. Her accuracy and ability to describe them in detail convinced me of her psychic abilities.

Nanci then picked up one of the pictures and began talking about Ryan. She stated that his cause of death had been self directed and that a series of disappointments had led up to his suicide; she listed those in detail: loss of his girlfriend, an argument or altercation between him and a group of friends, problems at work. She said that Ryan didn't feel as though he fit in anywhere. Those issues and the anger he held inside, had contributed to his rash decision to take his life.

She told me that Ryan had been looking for an instant solution to his problems. He told her that he was trying to be pro-active. Ryan felt that his life was out of control and this was his way of controlling it. Then Nanci looked at me and told me that he wanted to talk to me. She said, "I wasn't going to do any channeling today because it takes so much out of me," but she was willing to make an exception because he was so insistent. She told me that he had something important he wanted to say to me *himself*.

I'd never been to anyone that channeled spirits, so I had no idea of what to expect. She explained that in channeling, the spirit has the ability to speak *through* her. This is helpful to the sitter (me) because they often use their own mannerisms when speaking, and this makes it easier to identify them. I was bewildered by the turn of events simply because it all seemed just too bizarre to me. Losing Ryan had opened me up to try many different things, but I feared that this might be just a little too far off the beaten path — even for me. Instead of panicking, I took a deep breath and reminded myself that in the aftermath of suicide; little was left that could truly shock me. A few seconds later, Nanci began...

The first thing said to me was, "Mom, I love you, I love you, I love you...*I'm sorry, I'm sorry, I'm sorry*. I just wanted the pain to stop. I screwed up. I was just so ashamed...I was afraid of going to jail. I just hate what I did to everyone..." I was dumbfounded, and immediately relieved that I had followed through with the reading. My first request had been addressed ("Tell me that you're sorry"), and I felt my earlier reservations about the channeling fall to the wayside.

Ryan went on to say he was safe, and that I shouldn't worry about him. As I looked on, Nanci took her arms and opened them as wide as she could until they were almost touching behind her back. This action was followed by, "I love you soooo much." This gesture was exactly like the one Ryan had always used when asked, "How much do you love me?" To demonstrate his amount of love he would extend his arms exactly the way Nanci just had, straining to reach further, squinting his eyes, and screwing his face up in the process. For me, the familiarity of this action helped confirm Ryan's presence.

The reading continued, "Please apologize to everyone for me — I hope they can forgive me. I've got my head together now Mom...What's done is done...I can't change the past. I'm around you a lot Mom, like an angel on your shoulder. I'm never far; just call and I'll be there. *We'll*

*be talking in your mind of course — so don't think you're going crazy...*We're square now Mom — Right?"

My second request had been delivered ("Clarify that you are the one I keep hearing in my mind")! Ryan had cleverly followed up by asking a question himself. It was just like him to solicit confirmation on a job well done. He had indeed addressed both of the items I had been drilling him on for two weeks, and deserved to be answered. In my overwhelmed state I struggled to find my voice. It took a few seconds before I was able to say — "Yes Bud...we're square now."

The channeling portion ended, but the reading continued a little while longer and it provided some good information. At the end of the session, Nanci handed me the cassette tape of our reading. I thanked her and gratefully accepted the hug she offered to me. I was in a daze from my first channeling experience and found myself amused, but grateful, to have made contact with Ryan once again. This event reminded me that life isn't about the destination, it's about the journey, and this unexpected twist had just made mine a lot more interesting. I left feeling happy and satisfied. My questions had been answered, *and then some...*

PART THREE

RECOGNIZING THE SIGNS

25

LOVES ME LIKE A ROCK

SOON AFTER MY READING with Nanci, I wrote a poem for Ryan. I titled it *The Voice*:

> The Voice, it spoke inside of me — I heard it, soft and clear.
>   Urging me Up —
>   Urging me Out —
>   Pulling me forward.
>
> It told me you were Safe — It said that you were Happy....
>   It stated: "He is Free."
>   Free from worry —
>   Free from Pain —
>   Free from the Burdens that plagued him here on Earth.
>
> Somehow I knew — *The Voice inside was YOU.*
>   Lifting me Up —
>   Pulling me Out —
>   Urging me down the path of life, while I bear the grief of loss.
>
> Sweet Ryan — I am so happy that *you are Safe* —
>   So Relieved that *you are free of your Burdens* —
>   So grateful that I can — Hear YOU:
>   Inside my head, inside my heart
>   Where our Souls can Touch, Even if We can't....

-S.E.G. 2004

I was so very grateful to have experienced all that I had, but true to human nature, I could not help wishing for more. At this phase, I had become used to the dull ache that lived inside of me. I still longed to see Ryan, and made this request each and every day. I have read dozens of stories describing how others have experienced visits from their loved ones while fully conscious. I'd actually seen my deceased grandmother once, so I knew that it was possible.

I believe my grandma's visit had been prompted by my health issues. The night before a scheduled trip to the hospital, I had gotten up, unable to sleep. I'd walked into the kitchen and opened the blinds that covered the sliding glass door facing the back yard. There she was, sitting at the table on our deck in her housedress. She looked at me and said, "It's not your time," then she was gone.

I ran into our bedroom and shook Joe. I asked him if I was awake. He looked at me like I had a screw loose and told me, "Yes, you're awake and now I am too." This confirmed that I hadn't been dreaming. He then rolled over and went back to sleep as I stood there in wonder. I couldn't stop myself from hoping that one day I would see Ryan like this too.

I was greatly pacified by the few spirit light photos he'd given us. Having physical proof of Ryan's contact had become paramount to me. Those nagging doubts were much easier to silence when I could hold proof in my hands. Ryan always does his best to help me, and that spring, following Nanci's reading, he found a new way to provide me with physical proof that was meaningful.

In the spring of 2004, we planned another home project. We decided to put more concrete and paving bricks in the backyard by the pool and got a bid to pave our driveway as well. This project required moving our landscaping rocks, something we had already done several times.

I have this thing about rocks — I love them, and we have plenty. They border all around our house and pool. I'd spent hours rearranging them to accommodate our growing home several times. I would tell Ryan and Katie that rocks were an art form, to which they would roll their eyes at me and then quickly hide to escape from helping me move them.

Ryan would always cave and end up pitching in to help. I spent a lot of time thinking about him and his helping hands that Memorial Day weekend as I moved the rocks yet again. Because of the holiday, I had 4 days off and I spent all of them in the backyard finishing the stone removal so that our cement could be poured the following week. I kept the radio on as I worked and many of my favorite "Ryan songs" were played. This always prompted me to talk aloud to him as I toiled away at my task.

On Monday, I found that only a small stretch of about 7 or 8 feet remained to be removed. I sat back on my heels and pulled on my gloves, speaking to Ryan as I prepared for my work. I said, "Thanks for keeping me company this weekend Cowboy — I could always count on you to help me with my rocks. I felt you with me each day, and I really appreciated how you let me know you were here by playing all of our songs. I love you Ryan…" I reached down and picked up the first rock of the day. I looked at it in disbelief and let out a loud cry. I could hardly believe my own eyes! There in my hand was a rock, shaped exactly like a heart.

Joe had heard me cry out and he came around the corner to see what all the commotion was about. Tears streamed down my face as I held my rock out to him. He looked at it and then pulled me close. He said, "Ryan just wants you to know how much he loves you honey." I sobbed and thanked my son over, and over again. I explained to him that I was shedding happy tears and that I was completely thrilled by the beautiful gift he had given me.

I now have over 30 heart rocks that I keep in glass vases in my study. Each one has a special meaning to me. Over 90% of them have materialized from the landscaping in my own yard. Even though I have searched and searched for them there, they only seem to appear when I need them the most. They are Ryan's way of telling me, "I'm here Momma."

That summer, while lounging by the pool, a song came on the radio that I had long forgotten about. It fits my "heart rock" gifts perfectly and Ryan quickly added it to my personal playlist. It's a song by Paul Simon entitled "Loves me like a Rock," and every time I hear it played I can't help but think of Ryan and my lovely heart rock collection. I guess this is just one more circumstance where music says it best.

(left) My first "Heart Rock"

(below) My collection of Heart Rocks — still growing!

Most of these were found in the landscaping around our home.

26

HELPING KATIE

KATIE FINISHED HER FIRST year at SVSU. We packed her things up and moved her home for the summer. She was hired at a local bank and seemed to enjoy the work. Her degree was going to be in business, and working in the banking industry exposed her to a variety of possible career choices. She was seeing the new grief counselor and seemed to be doing a little better. I had adjusted to the empty nest, but was really looking forward to having her home with me for the next 4 months.

Seeing Katie on a daily basis gave me a better idea of where she was in the grieving process. She never said anything about her brother or her pain unless she was asked. It was rare for her to offer any information voluntarily. A memory that burns in my mind took place the day after Ryan died. Katie and I were standing in the kitchen together when something was said about parents and the burden of their grief. I recall her turning to me and saying, "What about me? I lost my big brother." I had taken her in my arms and told her, "Yes you did Baby, and it hurts like hell doesn't it?" Then and there, I made a vow to never let her grief get lost in the shuffle.

People do focus on the parents when a child dies, but in truth, siblings often know one another the best. Our childhoods are spent sharing secrets and building memories with our brothers and sisters. They help to shape the history of our lives. They know the other side of us that exists, the unrestricted part that we are free to express when away from the prying eyes of our parents. When Ryan died he took the majority of those memories with him, and Katie was feeling that void.

Sibling grief is different than parental grief, but it can be just as intense. Their pain gets trapped inside of them because they don't want to be responsible for saying or doing something that might make their parents anguish worse. They lose their mothers and fathers to grief, and then often struggle on their own to deal with the chaos death leaves behind.

Surviving children also seem to approach things with a larger-than-life exuberance. I believe the invisible weight of their dead sibling makes them feel the need to experience everything, not only for themselves, but also for their lost loved one. Parental paranoia adds to the burden they bear and this makes being a surviving child possibly the most difficult job of all.

I could only imagine what Katie was feeling, so I did what I could to try and understand. In an effort to help her I purchased a book entitled *The Empty Room* by Elizabeth DeVita-Raeburn. It is about a sibling, recovering from the loss of a sibling. I wanted to show her that she wasn't alone in her pain, and hoped it would provide her with some helpful ways to deal with the uniqueness of sibling grief. Reading wasn't something Katie did a lot of, but she made her way through the book at her own pace, and commented afterwards that it had been a useful tool for her.

I wanted to help my daughter, so I tried to share with her the tools that had helped me. I booked an appointment for us to see Elaine a few days before the second anniversary of Ryan's death. I had taken Katie once before and it had helped her greatly. She had cried afterwards and told me, "Thanks for bringing me to talk to my brother, Mom." I was hoping he would provide her with a few new personal things to let her know he was still near, and watching over her.

I explained to Katie how I had been prepping Ryan for our visits together. She told me to do it for this reading and to be sure to tell him to, "give me good shit" and not to waste her time. Following her orders, I told him exactly that, both at the cemetery and in his room as I spoke into the mirror. I was looking forward to experiencing what he had to deliver.

It's different, and I believe difficult, for Elaine to read when there are two "sitters" in the room. We all have our own energy and it's possible to get them crossed when you share the same space. This happened in our reading that day, and Katie became irritated. She was there to talk to Ryan, but Elaine kept getting a lot of things that were for me. Poor Elaine, I knew she could feel Katie's agitation.

Three quarters of the way through the reading, Elaine stopped and started to rub her finger. She looked at Katie and said, "I'm getting some pain in my finger — did Ryan cut himself there?" The color drained from Katie's face. She turned to me and said, "That's good shit Mom." It was indeed. As I wrote earlier, Katie and I had both noticed the cut on Ryan's finger that day at the funeral home when we'd said our good-byes. We had both thought about putting a band aid on it. Instantly, we knew that this was what he was trying to communicate.

Ryan gave a few more personal details to substantiate that he was watching over her. Facts about Katie's sorority sisters and her antics at SVSU were given and she relaxed some. Afterwards, in the car, we both agreed that the "cut finger" had been well worth the trip. The reading wasn't what Katie had hoped for, but the information provided had been accurate and personal. Once again, we don't always get what we want, but we do get what we need.

A few days after the reading, Ryan's death date arrived. Everyone has their own "scent" and we can always smell Ryan when he visits us. I smelled him in the basement that morning, before I noticed that the door to the storage compartment under the stairs was open. To get our attention he'd opened that door. We keep our luggage there for storage, so unless we were packing for a trip it remains closed. The only time I had ever seen the storage door opened like that, had been the morning

of his suicide. I had gone downstairs to kiss the kids goodbye that morning, before I left for work. As I headed back up the stairs, I noticed that it was open. Curious, but in a hurry to get on the road, I had simply closed it and left. It was there, that the police believed he'd hidden the rifle. Since the suicide, he has opened this door several times, but only on June 28th — the day of his death.

On Ryan's birthday, a week later, we repeated our tradition using balloons and fireworks to celebrate the day. I released my balloon and watched it soar into the sunset. When I did, I noticed that in the sky above — a perfect crescent moon and a single solitary star were shining in an otherwise starless sky. The picture this presented was exactly like the design of the ring I wear in his memory. How perfect to experience this heavenly visual on his birthday! This sign comforted me in a way that nothing else in this world could, and I made it a point to thank him for acknowledging our special symbol.

Ryan had started out the third year of our grief with some significant and creatively delivered miracles. It reassured me to know that he was still watching over us. Unbeknownst to us, we were all about to turn a very important corner. Before "year three" was over, we would all experience miracles that enabled us to better embrace the signs he was sending. The next lesson on our agenda was clear: *BELIEVE*.

27

THE CHAISE

As we headed into the third year of recovery, I could feel the unspoken words of my peers — thinking that I should be getting over it and dwelling less on my loss. It was only a select few that made me feel that way, but I could see the number of them growing as the months and years passed. If they only knew how much effort it took just to get myself out of bed in the morning. How I was forced to swallow my grief each and every day just so they would feel more comfortable. It hurt to look at their grown sons and family photos. I tried not to resent them for having things that I would never again be able to enjoy. My family felt incomplete, and I didn't know when — or if — that void would ever leave us.

I learned to guard my conversation around the "get over it" individuals; they thought they were helping me by ignoring the situation, but what it really did was to sink me deeper into my despair. I didn't have the luxury of forgetting the reality of our circumstances. I needed them to understand that just because our child was dead didn't mean that we'd stopped thinking of him or that we'd lost the ability to remember the things that he'd said and done.

When their children go off to college, will they stop talking about them? If someone does something funny or familiar that reminds them of their children, won't they mention that? The only difference between us was that my child wouldn't be making any new memories for me to share, but I had plenty of good ones stored away. You can't explain things like this; it is too difficult for most people to comprehend. I just had to focus on the fact that healing was on my timetable — not theirs.

My grief had become more manageable, but there were still days when I just couldn't push it down. I let it out when I had to and always felt better for having done so, but for me the terminal guilt and physical longing I had for Ryan, kept everything somewhat raw. My coping skills enabled me to keep functioning, and it was a great relief to note that the emotional roller coaster we'd been riding on had slowed down some, which allowed more time for recovery.

My neighbor Charlene understood what I was going through. She has lost two children, both of whom I'd known growing up. She listened to me as I shared my thoughts and feelings with her. She was a role model for me and I truly looked up to her. I admired her strength and drew mine from her when I needed to. It wasn't until we headed into our third year of grieving that I shared one of my miracles with her. This one involved one of the chaises out by the pool.

A week or so before Ryan's death date I went out on the deck to have my nightly chat and a cigarette. I found that my gaze was being drawn to one of the chaise lounges near the pool. Staring at it triggered a memory I had of Ryan lying there the evening before the suicide...

That fateful night, I had been out by the pool fussing with the water testing kit when he'd wandered outside. Ryan had stopped at the chaise and then laid down on it. I finished with the pool and watched him with worry. He was so quiet, just laying there — not moving — his eyes fixed on the clouds above. I recalled telling him that I was going into the house to take care of some laundry if he wanted to come in and talk. I told him that I loved him and to stop worrying, that everything was going to be all right.

I cried as I stood there, remembering the events of that evening only three short years ago. I said aloud, "Every time I look at that chaise I think of you Ryan, and it just makes me so damn sad." I finished my smoke and went back into the house.

The next morning I woke up early and went outside with my coffee. I walked out toward the pool and noticed that the chaise in question was submerged in the water. I looked around to see if anything else had maybe blown in, but our towels still hung on the hooks outside the pool house and several plastic kiddie chairs were still upright and firmly in place. Everything was just as we had left it the night before, with the exception of the chaise.

I pulled it out of the pool and couldn't believe how heavy and awkward it was. After wrestling it out of the water, I knew that any wind from the night before wasn't even remotely capable of blowing that chaise in the pool. If it had — the kiddie chairs and beach towels would have went in too. Right then and there, I knew that it had to have been Ryan.

Evidently, he had heard me the night before, and watched me as I'd cried. Hurling it into the pool was something he would do to express his feelings. He'd say, "Just get rid of the damn thing if it makes you so sad." In my guts, I knew this was his way of expressing his frustration over the sadness of our situation. I took the time to check with Joe and Katie to see if they might have accidentally pushed it in, but the answer was "no" from both of them. I wasn't surprised.

A few days after sharing this incident with Charlene, I received a card from her. It had a beach chair on the front of it, and inside she'd written:

"Sally, I went to get my cards for this month and this card was staring at me. One lone chair...I had to get it for you especially after our conversation about Ryan's chair in the pool... It doesn't seem possible Jerry has been gone 5 years and Ryan 2 years. This week, I am taking it a day at a time. Don't know why, but it has been rough." *(Jerry is the son she lost and his death date falls in the same week as Ryan's.)

The Reason

Charlene's card touched me deeply and I kept it as a testament to the miracle I had shared with her. Her note reminded me that healing takes time. Our relationship helped me to see that supporting one another is what it's all about, and snagging a little hope from the stories of others doesn't hurt either.

2 8

FEATHER'S DAY

MY POWERS OF OBSERVATION grew as the intensity of my grief slowly subsided. This expanding awareness is what prompted me to take a second look at the feathers I'd been receiving. Since Ryan's death, there had been a steady stream of them. I'd come to accept that the feathers were little signs of encouragement from him, but had never taken the time to understand or fully appreciate their meaning.

Joe was the first to notice the feathers. A few days after the funeral he'd walked up to me with three blue jay feathers in his hand and said, "Here honey, I think these are from Ryan." I was too consumed with pain at the time to comprehend a possible link between Ryan and the feathers, but something must have clicked inside of me, because I did save them.

Throughout that summer and into the next, feathers seemed to materialize out of nowhere following moments of helplessness and despair. Because of Joe's comment, I was especially sensitive to them and always saved every feather I found. I love getting them, and they had a healing power over me that I can't explain.

Out of curiosity, I began asking family and friends if they ever found feathers. Their common response was "No." This is what compelled me to look more closely at when and where I found them. Late one afternoon I decided to go through the box of feathers that I kept on my dresser. As I held each one, I recalled the memory associated with it. It was during this time of silent contemplation that I suddenly felt the

urge to go to the book store. Time and experience had taught me to give into these sudden impulses because they usually turned up something worthwhile. This trip was no exception.

I didn't go to Borders, which was strange. I hardly ever go anywhere else, but on that day, I did. I went to a bookstore inside the mall and found myself wandering back to the Metaphysical section. I slowly trailed my index finger along the rows of books. Intuition was telling me that I would know it when I saw it, and I did.

I stopped abruptly when my gaze settled on a book entitled *Sacred Feathers* by Maril Crabtree. I took it from the shelf and began thumbing through it. Its contents literally floored me! It described, through the stories of others, that feathers were indeed signs from the other side. Receiving a feather can mean a variety of things, but their message is generally a positive one. Feathers are the messengers of opportunity, healing and hope. They are highly spiritual symbols of sacred power and carry a huge history.

I had found what I had come for and so I purchased the book. On a whim, I stopped at Borders on my way home to see if they carried a copy of *Sacred Feathers* in their store. They did not have it in stock, but offered to order it for me. This proved once again that my intuition had steered me in the right direction, and it thrilled me to know that following it had landed me a treasury of valuable information.

Reading this wonderful book opened another door inside of me. It explained that certain types or colors of feathers had a general meaning or message attached to them, providing the potential for Ryan to communicate much more that just "hello." It made me a little crazy to think of all I had missed by not comprehending their individual meanings earlier. Poor Ryan — I guess he just couldn't take my stupidity anymore, and so he'd led me to a book that could explain their meanings and significance. I visualized him doing the "happy dance," grinning from ear to ear, now that I finally got it. This was another lesson in awareness I was happy to have learned.

I love those feathers, they never fail to move me, and many of my favorite stories include them. It was through the feathers that I eventually understood my role as an interpreter for my family. I was more open to receiving Ryan's signs and cognizant of their meanings, which made it my job to communicate and explain the miracles that came my way. Pointing out the specifics related to these events would hopefully heighten their awareness too. If Ryan used the same signs to reach out to them, then the knowledge I was sharing would enable them to recognize his efforts and receive those miracles for themselves.

One of my favorite feather stories involved being an interpreter for Joe. The last time Joe and Ryan had golfed together was in June of 2002, at the Country Club's annual Father/Son tournament, only weeks before Ryan died. That day had been cold and rainy, but they had come home happy as clams. When I'd asked Ryan how they'd played, he'd said, "We shot like crap Mom, but we were the best dressed team on the course!" This made us all laugh because Joe's gift that year had been rain gear, and he had worn it proudly to the tournament that day.

On Father's Day of 2004, Joe went golfing late in the afternoon at the Country Club with a few of his friends. It was tough on him, but he saw it as an opportunity to remember that special day two short years ago. I didn't see the feathers in Joe's van until a few days after the fact. We were driving down to my dad's house when I noticed three jumbo feathers on his dash. I picked them up, commented on their size, and asked him where he had found them. Joe looked at me and said, "I found them on the course the other day and saved them for you, Honey. I keep forgetting to bring them into the house."

I looked at my husband and asked him to tell me what day *specifically* that had been. He told me that he had found them on Sunday,

Father's Day. I laughed as I held them out to him. I said, "These aren't for me Joe, they're for you — from Ryan — Happy Father's Day." The look on his face was priceless. I will remember it for as long as I live. It was joy, love, surprise and a tinge of disbelief mixed all together. He took them from me and for the first time, considered that the feathers may have been for him. When it finally sunk in you couldn't remove the smile from my husband's face.

The most powerful feather story I have involved my brother David. He is the Executive Vice President of a logistics company and a very busy man. Most of his time is spent traveling, so his cell phone and laptop are instrumental for conducting his daily business and maintaining contact with his family. While at work one day, I received a phone call from David. He was at the airport awaiting his flight and was killing time by checking his e-mails. He called to tell me that he had just forwarded something to me that I needed to check out. I could tell from the tone of his voice that it was something important, so I logged into my mailbox and opened his message.

His note to me said:

"Sal, I thought that you might like to see this message. Basically, we had a container delivered to a customer that had feathers in the container. Our customer does not import anything to do with feathers. They import plastic bags. The two commodities loaded in the container prior to this were air conditioners and rayon/cotton fabrics. The source of the feathers is unknown. Although this is an indirect path to me, I wanted to share this story with you. I just thought maybe this was Ryan trying to send me a sign also. The attached file is a digital picture of the feathers found in the container."

I opened the file and could hardly believe my own eyes. There in the photo was a pile of feathers lying in the container. Of course, this was Ryan trying to get David's attention! How else would you get a busy executive to notice a feather unless you sent him one in an e-mail? I had shared many of my stories with my brother, so he was able to recognize the underlying message when he received it. I was impressed and very proud that Ryan had gone to such lengths to give my brother this sign. It was by far one of his very best efforts in communication.

I called my brother back and we had a few minutes to discuss the e-mail before he had to board his plane. He explained to me that these types of messages are generally handled by his staff, and hardly ever make it to his level of management. The fact that he had received this one was a miracle in itself. David had been deeply affected by Ryan's suicide and I knew the closeness of their relationship was the reason why my son was reaching out to him. It was important to him that David found hope and healing too.

Ryan's elaborate and sophisticated scheme to communicate his message of love to my brother had been successful. I looked again at the e-mail that David had forwarded to me. It made me swell with pride; *my son did that*...AWESOME.

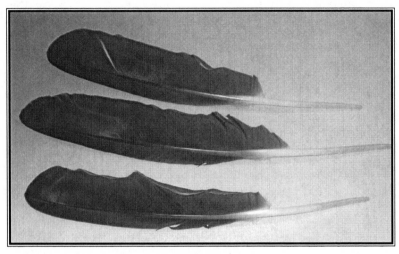

Joe – Feathers for Father's Day

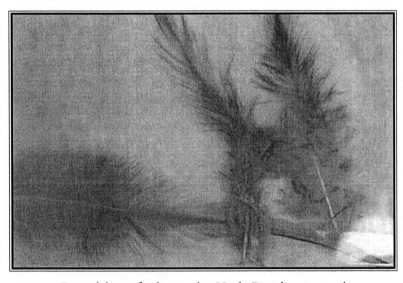

Ryan delivers feathers to his Uncle David – via email

29

SEND IN THE COURIER

MOST OF THE TIME I was right on point when it came to receiving Ryan's messages, but there were occasions when my emotional state blocked his efforts. This didn't happen often, but when it did Ryan always had a backup plan, and this usually involved my friend Lori.

Actually, Lori set herself up to be Ryan's personal courier. One day, she accompanied me to the cemetery and told him "Ryan, you can use me anytime you need to if it will help your Mom." Her heartfelt offer made it easy for him to engage her services, leaving the door between them wide open. Ryan's creative approach in delivering the miracles was increasing, and in mid November of 2004, he used something completely different and highly innovative to enlist Lori's help.

Katie had come home for a visit that weekend. I had put up a new wallpaper border in Ryan's bedroom, and was rearranging his furniture and hanging pictures when Katie wandered in. It was Sunday and she was getting ready to head back up to college. She wanted to discuss bringing her new boyfriend home for a visit. She had been to his mothers' house a few times already, and now she wanted to invite him to spend a weekend at ours. Before she extended the invitation, she wanted to know what the sleeping arrangements would be.

I told Katie that her boyfriend could sleep in Ryan's room. She did not react well to this. Katie told me it would be too scary for her to have him sleep in her brother's room. I told her that was silly because I had just spent the whole weekend redecorating it. I reminded her that everything in the room was brand new, so it wasn't as if he would be touching Ryan's things. I also told her that I thought it would be a good idea to have someone else sleep in there — that it might get us all over a big hump. I told her, "Your brother is gone and we all need to move on."

Katie just stood there with a horrified look on her face, so I added that she could always sleep in the daybed upstairs, and the boyfriend could sleep in her room. From her perspective, this was a much more acceptable solution, so we agreed on that arrangement and ended our discussion.

Just for the record — I wasn't myself when we had this conversation. Spending all that time in Ryan's room had been difficult. At that point, it took all of my strength to keep from having a meltdown in front of her. I had avoided crying by using anger to keep my tears at bay; otherwise, I would never have said, "we all need to move on." It was a cruel thing to say, because it made me sound like I wanted to forget Ryan and nothing could have been further from the truth.

Katie left soon after our discussion to drive back to school. Saying goodbye to her was the last straw. I felt my sorrow crest, and before her car even left the driveway, I was deep into the black hole of grief. I spent the rest of the night in there and it took a lot of work to extract myself. It took an additional day to fully recuperate, but I was feeling much better when I got to work on Tuesday.

I always start my work day by reading my e-mails. When I opened my mailbox, I discovered a note from my friend Lori there. She said:

Hi Miss Sally,

I wanted to tell you — I've been thinking about Ryan this morning...when I was in the shower, and still not awake, I realized I was kind of daydreaming about him. The thoughts were just random thoughts, not sad, not happy — for some reason I was thinking about the mail box (you put up) at his grave site, and how that was a line to him and heaven...Not sure what it means — but when I realized I was thinking of him, I thought — I should tell Sally — maybe she knows something? There you have it — sorry if it seems a little "crazy" — but hey — I think we both know we're off our rockers...Lori"

Receiving this note from her was exciting! It meant that she was somehow tuned into my misery via Ryan. I sent an e-mail response off to her, telling her about my meltdown and that the past few days had been rough. I told her: "...he's worried about me, and he knows you're here, you're sensitive — He's calling in the troops — YOU..."

She sent me a second e-mail later that morning. *This one completely blew me away...*

"Sal,

Ryan does channel his thoughts through me when he wants to reach you. I am 100% convinced of this — now more than ever. You see — it wasn't logical thoughts — something didn't trigger me to think of him this time. That does happen; when I see someone that looks like him or someone asks how you are doing...I'll remember him and think of him. These thoughts come to me in kind of a dream like fashion — nothing triggered them...I'm telling you, they come directly from him when he needs me to reach you for him.

I find this fascinating — I'm thrilled I can receive these messages. Now I'm going to think hard on what thoughts floated in my head — they were just that — dream like thoughts.

I'll work backward because once I pictured the mailbox, my thoughts of telling you took me out of my dreamy state and they became more logical...

I thought of his room — how you redecorated it so nice — the red roses — and for some reason I thought about my staying in that room...I thought about your Katie, wondering if I would be "afraid" by staying in Ryan's room and I reassured her there was nothing to be afraid of. I got the idea that he (Ryan) is mad now — at himself — that he has just realized the "finality" of what he did and how that continues to hurt all of you, mostly you. I got the idea he's angry with himself — but it's kind of like the anger stage we go through when someone dies — almost as if he's going through the mourning process for himself...

I hope this helps you Sally — I would never want to say something that hurts you, but I told myself I would always pass along what he sends. I will tell you that I always slightly hesitate because I want to make sure it's something from him and not my own head. You confirmed for me that he was trying to reach you when you said you've had some bad days. I think when you're struggling he has a hard time reaching you, and has to come to me as an alternative...

Ryan truly is a wonderful son Sally — this must take a great deal of effort on his part, to try and take care of you like he has, to show his love and reach (out to) you from across time and place — We learn from this. I'm thinking this all means he needs you to help him right now, huh Sal?"

It was truly unbelievable that Ryan had been able to feed the conversation I'd had with Katie (about her boyfriend staying in his room) to Lori in a "daydream". It felt so crazy, but it was true. I called her on the telephone after receiving her second e-mail and explained to her the facts behind her daydream in the shower that morning. Lori found it to be just as incredulous as I had when I read her email. This was completely new territory for us both.

I found it hard to believe that two everyday, mid-western mothers (nothing special about us) were capable of having such a truly amazing experience. Did this type of thing really happen? Evidently, the answer was yes, because it had just happened to both of us, and it had been phenomenal!

I went to the cemetery that night after thinking about a few of the things Lori had pointed out to me. It was possible that Ryan missed us too, and he needed to know that I hadn't meant to hurt him by saying "we need to move on." At the cemetery, I tried to reassure him that he would always have a place in our hearts and family; that death had not changed the importance of the role he played in our lives. I made it clear that I was only trying to move our family forward, but that healing from our grief would never mean we were forgetting him. I told him, "We'll work through this together Ryan — as a family."

I was still his mother, and he was still my son. I reached out to comfort him as he had done so many times for me over the past months since his death. It felt good to know that he still needed me, and even better to know that I could give him the help he sought. Mothers need to be needed and this was no exception. It was a bittersweet lesson, but a valuable one nonetheless. I had to work within the confines of my situation, but with the right attitude — it was doable. His incredible miracle had made it so.

30

DREAMS AND RAINBOWS

RYAN MUST HAVE BEEN pleased with Lori's ability to convey his messages because early in the spring of 2005, he decided to give her another. Lori called me from Florida where she was on vacation with her family. Her voice was filled with excitement and she could hardly contain her enthusiasm as she described to me a dream she'd been given the night before.

Lori told me that I had been in her dream. Looking peaceful and serene, I had walked up to her with a book in my hands. The book was thin and dark blue in color. It was bigger; really more like a portfolio. I handed the book to Lori. She took it from me and opened it. Lori explained that looking at the pages of this book, was more like looking into a window; as if the scene before her were "alive," kind of like a movie.

Within the open pages, she saw Ryan. He was wearing a suit, and as she continued to gaze into the scene in front of her, she keenly observed that he was also moving slightly. Lori had the perception that this was an older, more mature Ryan, not the youth she had previously known. If she'd had to guess, she'd say that he appeared to be about 30 or so, this was because his forehead was visibly wrinkled in conjunction with the crow's-feet at the corners of his eyes.

An odd light poured forth from the open pages. She said it was like sunlight, but it wasn't so bright that you couldn't look at it. The light from the book made her feel as if she were a part of the book itself, but at the same time was conscious of the fact that she wasn't.

Lori said that there was no speaking, but telepathy was a part of the experience. Throughout this dream, she had an overall feeling of peace and contentment. The unspoken message she received was that I would get through the window to actually become a part of the scene it portrayed, when this happened, she wouldn't have to worry about me anymore.

I was enthralled with Lori's dream. I had read something about the moving, window like pages she had described in *Journey of Souls*, by Michael Newton, PH.D. In that text it described them as "life books" where souls can review their past (and sometimes get glimpses of their future) life lessons.

I was at a loss when it came to understanding what the "older" aged Ryan meant. (This mystery would be solved later — by yet another miracle.) The overall message this dream had to deliver was not fully realized until I began writing this book. I categorize these types of miracles as "scavenger hunts," because it takes a series of signs and realizations before you can see or understand the bigger picture or complete message they are meant to deliver. They take time and effort, but are so worth it in the end.

I decided to tell this story because it is a perfect example of why it is so important to keep track of all loose "puzzle pieces." There will be signs that we can't explain or comprehend at the time they are received, but there is always a reason why we receive them, so they should never be disregarded or dismissed. They will eventually reveal their purpose when the timing is right. Sometimes it is a matter of having the proper amount of knowledge or life experience to understand them. Like the feathers, they will usually disclose a broader understanding when revisited.

Dreams are a whole other subject matter; the important thing to bear in mind about them is that they have a message to deliver. Vivid dreams like these are sometimes a preview, to future people/events/realizations. Always pay attention to the details, and write down those that stand out the most. These are dreams, not reality, so not every detail should be taken literally. It is just one more form of communication spirits can use, and being aware of their importance can make a differ-ence in your healing experience.

At that time, I just appreciated Lori's dream for what it was — another point of contact from Ryan. I filed the loose puzzle pieces away for later scrutiny. It helped to ease the pain of my grief and that was all I cared about. The miracles were helping me to better understand *where* and *how* Ryan was. This was important, because ultimately it was my mission to answer those questions. Pursuing the answers is what kept me going, but in conjunction with my day-to-day grief, it could also be quite draining.

Several weeks after Lori's dream, I found myself in Ryan's room hav-ing another meltdown. It had come upon me out of nowhere and the suddenness of it proved to be untimely, because Katie was home. To shield her from the storm I could feel building inside of me, I'd encour-aged her to go to Target to pick up the items she'd seen in a recent ad. When she left, I went straight to Ryan's room and it was there that I unleashed my squall of emotions.

At this point in the game, I'd acquired the skills needed to extract myself from the black hole at will. So after my torrent of tears was released, I managed to collect myself and went outside to further re-group and to have a smoke. Out on the deck, I thanked the angels, God, and Ryan for watching over me and for giving me the strength to keep moving forward.

It had been raining for weeks, and I attributed my blue mood to the lousy weather and the lack of sunshine. I told Ryan it would make me feel better if he could give me a sign to let me know he was still there. I men-tioned that maybe he could give me a rainbow, but then said "no" fearing that would be too obvious because of all the rain. I needed a sign that I could be sure was *really* from him. So I said, "Well, you think of something Buddy — I'll know it's from you." Then I headed inside to take a shower.

Shortly after that, Katie came home. I was still taking my shower

when she blew into the bathroom and said, "I'm home Mom. I didn't find anything at the store, but I took a picture of a rainbow for you... When you get out (of the shower), I'll show it to you. It was stretched right across the highway on my way home — it was so cool!"

I thought I was going to faint. I stood motionless behind the shower curtain and let silent tears fall as I quietly mouthed a "thank-you" to my son. Katie was completely oblivious to the beautiful miracle she had just delivered. Ryan had found a special way to deliver *my rainbow*, and as always, it let me know, "I'm right here Momma..."

31

FROGS AND HERONS

In May of 2005, I made the following journal entry:

"I'm tired. Over the past few months, I've tried to pinpoint the cause of my fatigue. I considered several possibilities: age, early menopause, poor diet, and lack of exercise. I decided to tackle each probable cause, one by one, expecting that through the process of elimination I would be able to determine the primary source of my exhaustion.

I went to the doctor for blood work, started the Weight Watchers program to monitor my eating habits, and hired a personal trainer at the gym. Six months later, *I'm still tired.*

I took a long hard look at myself and made my own diagnosis — Extreme Fatigue from Grief. The problem of course, is there are no pills I can take; no food I can eat, and no place that I can go to cure it. The intensity with which I love my son is causing this condition, and I fear that it is leading me into terminal despair.

This proposes a problem. How does one carry on? How long am I destined to struggle along the pathway of sorrow?"

These were good points to ponder, but unfortunately, they weren't anything I had the answers to. I had been working hard on my grief, using my tools and applying the knowledge gained from the lessons, I'd been given. This had helped me tremendously, but clearly — I needed a break. It was then that I decided to take a "vacation" from my grief.

I ran this by my friend Judie one day and told her that my intention was not to think about Ryan or my sadness for an entire week. I explained that it was an experiment, designed to see if I could give myself a well deserved break from the chronic pain of my grieving. It was my hope that this vacation would help to renew and energize me.

Judie was supportive of my efforts; although I'm quite sure, she was a little leery of my overall expectations. Like any good friend she went along with my plan and afterward I was honest enough to tell her that although I had been able to keep my thoughts of Ryan and my grief at bay, the vacation had not left me feeling as revitalized as I had hoped.

I did learn something valuable from my experiment though. I learned that I had the ability to control my thoughts for an extended period, and this provided me with a new way to *manage* my grief, which was a huge step in the right direction.

The Science of Mind (aka Religious Science) philosophy is "Change your thinking — Change your life" and it was Norman Vincent Peale that stated, "Change your thoughts and change your world." Controlling thought isn't easy to do. It takes a lot of work, but by now, I was used to that.

I made it a daily practice. I knew that I wasn't going to stop thinking about my son, but remembering him didn't always have to make me sad either. When Ryan popped into my thoughts, I would make a conscious effort to think of something wonderful or funny about him. I stayed with that happy thought for a moment or two and then would let it go, re-adjusting my focus to the present moment. It didn't work every time, but it was a vast improvement nonetheless. Ryan must have been proud of my efforts, because he found a new way to reward and encourage my progress.

The third year of our grieving was winding down, but the summer's heat was in full swing. I was making frequent trips to the cemetery because I needed to water the fresh flowers that were planted there. My mother plants colorful annuals at Ryan's gravesite each spring, and my job is to keep everything healthy and well pruned. I enjoyed the quiet time I spent there while watering and performing my gardening duties.

It was during one of my watering trips that I decided to clean out Ryan's mailbox. Family and friends would often leave cards and mementos at his gravesite. In an effort to keep those things from being scattered about the cemetery, and to preserve the sentiment with which they'd been given, I'd installed a small mailbox over Ryan's headstone. Every month or so, I would check its contents and clean out some of the older items to store at home.

After watering that day, I lifted the lid of the mailbox and peered inside. I was amazed to see that among the cards and keepsakes sat a very large toad. The mailbox sat off the ground a good two feet and its heavy, metal lid kept it closed. I found no holes or openings that could have possibly provided outside entry; it was a mystery to me as to how the toad had gotten inside.

We stared at each other for a second or two and then I reached inside and took the toad out. I held it up to my face and gazed at it closely. The toad sat quietly in the palm of my hand and I found myself talking to it. I said, "Ryan, I like to think that this is you — something I can touch and hold." I gently stroked it with my finger and then without thinking twice, I planted a little kiss on the top of its head. This made me feel happy, so I laughed and let myself enjoy the glow it put on my day. I held the toad a little longer and then I set it on the grass and watched as it hopped away.

A week later, I dared to open the mailbox again, and discovered a frog inside! This one was much smaller and a little more active than the toad I'd found before. The frog jumped out of my hand as soon as I pulled it out of the mailbox. But when it landed in the grass, it just sat there staring at me. I laughed with glee and once more inspected the mailbox to see if I could discover how the frogs were getting inside. My second investigation turned up nothing.

Due to the mysterious appearances of the frogs and toad, watering the flowers at the cemetery became a lot more interesting. Over the course of the next several weeks, I rescued a few more from the confines of the mailbox. It was always a different amphibian; they were never the same shape or size. I couldn't figure out *why* I was finding them in there.

I shared several of these stories with Barrie, Judie, and my friend Lori. They all found it curious that the frogs would climb inside the mailbox when it was so hot outside. It had to be even hotter in that metal box! Barrie jokingly suggested that I hook up a camera at the cemetery; thinking that if we could figure out *how* they got inside, it would answer the question of *why*.

On Ryan's death date that year, my friend Lori went to the cemetery to place a floral arrangement she had made for him at the gravesite. She left me several messages that afternoon, both at work and at home. I caught up with Lori later that day. It was then that she told me her story. Lori said that along with the flowers, she had also brought a card for Ryan. When she lifted the lid of the mailbox to deposit the card, she had discovered a toad inside! She laughed when she described to me how it had startled her. Lori quickly shut the lid, afraid that it would get out before I had a chance to find it there. In an e-mail, she said:

> "...I'm telling you — when I saw that toad sitting there — looking up at me — I knew he had to have a greater meaning... Without a doubt, Ryan set him there as a message

to get you started down yet another road to a higher level of awareness and understanding...

I really do feel better because of that toad — funny huh? It felt tangible and real — that connection from Ryan...I'm happy for you Sal..."

Lori did some research on the internet and later that evening sent me another e-mail that had the name of a book, by author Penn Kemp. She said:

"Sal...I knew it! There is a meaning behind Ryan putting the toad in the mailbox...there is a book called *Kiss of Toad* — below is some of the book review..."

Lori had attached the book review and I read it. I was fascinated, but still unsure of what to make of it all. I searched the internet looking for a website where I could purchase the book, but when I didn't have any luck in doing so; I went back to the author's website and sent her a message from there.

The next day, I received the authors reply. She told me that the book I was looking for was still not published, but she suggested that I order a play of the same story titled *The Epic of Toad and Heron*. She provided the ordering information as well. I responded with my shipping information and then told her:

"I lost my son three years ago on June 28th. He started (by) leaving me feathers...three months ago he started leaving toads in a little mailbox I keep at his gravesite. My friend Lori was convinced there was some connection/message there. She found your book online and the review sounded just like the spiritual journey I have been on since Ryan crossed over. I just

follow my intuition these days — that has been the best route...
so I am going to read your play...Just a little tidbit as to how I
came to know your writing. I guess there is something there my
son Ryan wants me to know."

I mailed my check for the play. About two weeks later, I found yet
another frog sitting in Ryan's mailbox. Joe and I went out for dinner that
night and I told him about the new frog while at the restaurant. On our
drive home, he told me that he'd shared my frog stories with some of his
close friends. They had told him that they were just tree frogs, and that
they could have gotten into the mailbox easily.

Joe's words cut me like a knife. Instantly, I felt sickened and sad. I
started to cry. I told him that they were not tree frogs; they didn't even
resemble a tree frog. Joe was surprised and shocked by my reaction.
Truthfully, I was too...I had no idea how much those frogs meant to me
until someone tried to explain them away.

It was raining when we got home. I stayed outside and sat quietly under the covered part of the deck. I stared blankly at the pouring
rain, wondering what to do. Inside me a battle was raging. It was a war
between what *I felt to be true* and what *people wanted me to believe*. It
was then that I realized my faith was being tested. I had a choice: Was I
going to let someone take my hope from me, or was I going to stand up
for what I knew in my heart was the truth?

It didn't take long to make my choice; *I chose to believe in that which
gave me hope.* I was inspired to do so because of a quote I had recently
read in the newspaper, "Faith is to believe what we do not see; the reward
of this faith is to see what we believe" (Saint Augustine). I asked for a
sign that I had made the right choice, and then I went inside to get a
few things done.

The daily mail was lying on the kitchen table. Joe had brought it in while I was outside. I thumbed through it and noticed that a large mailing envelope was addressed to me. I was excited to see that the play, *The Epic of Toad and Heron* had arrived. I opened the package and pulled the play out so that I could flip through it. I wept when I saw that the author had taped a feather to the title page. Beneath the feather, she had graciously written a dedication and autographed my copy of her play. It said, "For Sally, in memory of Ryan, "Like circling suns," All the best, Penn Kemp." It was my sign...and a beautiful one at that. In my opinion, there's no better validation than a feather.

I read the play that evening and enjoyed it even more knowing I had been guided to read it. The foreword written for the play best describes the premise of the story:

> "Through an alchemical, ritualistic process, transformation is achieved — the princess becomes a heron, toad finds his true nature by joining and compromising with the heron. These transformations symbolize the finding of the lost selves within, the finding of the whole, true self."

The symbolism used in the play took me a long way when it came to understanding why Ryan was leaving me frogs at the cemetery. They represented the ability to grow and transform myself so I could rebuild my shattered life. I did additional research on the internet and found that historically frogs are a sign of transformation. Because of their three stages of growth (egg, tadpole, frog) they also symbolize resurrection and spiritual development. I discovered that there is also something referred to as "frog energy," and this energy is believed to create a link between the living and the dead.

Ryan delivered a second sign the following day to reinforce his message. I had been out doing errands and decided to stop at my sister

Stephanie's house to return something I'd borrowed. We were standing in her driveway talking when I noticed a large and graceful bird fly overhead. Stephanie and I watched as it landed in the creek that runs between my parent's and sister's property. She said, "Isn't it beautiful? It's a blue heron — weird place for it to call home — there's hardly any water in that creek, but it's been there for days."

My head almost snapped off my shoulders when she said "Heron." They are usually found along coastlines, in marshes, or near the shores of ponds or streams. It was indeed odd to see one in our little creek. I watched as it waded in the water, and realized that the timely appearance of this bird was a clear sign in itself. Due to the title and content of the play I had just received, it dawned on me that I should dig deeper into the symbolism of the heron.

Inadvertently, I typed in "crane-symbolism" while searching the internet for answers. This landed me on a S.O.S. (Survivors of Suicide) support group website. A story titled *Legend of the Crane* was posted there and it stated that, "*The powerful wings of the crane were believed to be able to convey souls up to paradise and to carry people to higher levels of spiritual enlightenment.*"

Herons share much of the same symbolism as cranes and other wading birds, so I figured the error in defining my search, as "crane" instead of "heron" wasn't important. The fact that this criteria had taken me to a S.O.S. website was meaningful and I took comfort in the message I had found there.

The best part about learning the symbolism behind the frogs and herons was the fact that this knowledge came after they had mysteriously appeared in my life, so it wasn't as if I knew what they represented and went out looking for them. With Lori's encouragement, I had searched for, and found their deeper meaning. This lesson had been designed to teach me that recovery meant transformation, and in my case, this included spiritual development.

I did a mental check and consulted my map. "Keep searching and you will find" was the direction I'd been given; it was good advice. If you don't take action, you'll never move beyond your grief. It doesn't really matter what sparks your quest for knowledge, what's important is that you keep pushing forward and allow your awareness to guide you to the next lesson. Frogs/toads, cranes/herons — what difference does it make where our lessons come from? What's important is that we grasp the messages they are designed to deliver.

"The Epic of Toad and Heron", (a play by Penn Kemp)
and her thoughtful dedication

32

A BUTTERFLY FOR JOE

It wasn't enough that I believed wholeheartedly in the miracles; I wanted Joe and Katie to believe in them too. It was as if I were still operating the boat to recovery alone, pointing out the miracles along the way to a host of observers. I didn't need observers, what I needed was *a crew*.

The miracles had opened Joe and Katie's eyes to the possibilities, but unless they could embrace the healing power the miracles provided, their struggle would remain unchanged. In order to get them to the next level, Ryan honed in on a more individual approach.

My husband loves golf — loves it. Ryan was wise to incorporate this in his plan and concentrated his efforts at the golf course to personalize Joe's miracle. To improve his odds, Ryan chose to deliver it during the Country Club's Annual Golf Invitational. Joe looks forward to this tournament each year, making it a golden opportunity; he is never more focused than when he's playing for a prize.

The Invitational is three days long. It starts on Thursday and finishes on Saturday. Joe and his partner were playing really well, and by Saturday, his game was "on fire." Joe headed for the course early that day, filled with confidence and enthusiasm. My plan was to spend the afternoon enjoying our pool while he finished golfing in the tournament.

I called my friend Michelle and invited her to join me poolside. I puttered around, pulling weeds and pruning plants while I awaited her arrival. It was a hot day, and I soon headed into the pool house for a bottle of water. It was then that a large Monarch butterfly flew up and started fluttering all around me. I had to laugh because it was so play-ful. It flew around my head and then followed me as I wandered back into the yard. Instinctively, I spoke to it saying "Hi Ryan. How are you? You look so beautiful today! Joe's golfing in the Invitational at the club. Why don't you wish him good luck? Love you Buddy..." The butterfly hung around and played with me for a little while longer, and then it flew away.

About an hour later, Michelle arrived. We hadn't seen each other in awhile and the conversation flowed as we attempted to get caught up. We were sitting on the pool steps in the shallow end, when the Monarch butterfly reappeared, only this time it started flying all around Michelle. She said, "Hi Ryan, just dropping by to say hello? Come and sit on my shoulder..." With that, the butterfly started landing all over her — on her thigh, chest, and arm. We both burst into laughter.

I asked her, "What made you call it Ryan?" She said it just felt like him, because it was "being a little pest." It was then I told her my story about playing with what appeared to be the very same butterfly, earlier that morning. We chuckled and marveled at our coincidental experi-ence, then moved on to other topics of conversation.

A few hours later Joe returned home. He was very excited and full of pride when he announced to us that he and his partner had won first place (in their flight) in the golf tournament! Joe made us all a cocktail and we toasted his big win. Michelle and I smiled politely as he began telling us, hole by hole, about his winning game...*blah, blah, blah golf.*

About 20 minutes into Joe's replay, Michelle noticed that it was get-ting late and she started packing up to leave. When Joe saw that part of his audience was exiting, he said, "Wait a minute, I've got one more story." He told us, "I was on the 16th hole, standing on the left side of the fairway lining up my shot...I went to take my swing and a big *orange butterfly* flew right into my swing path. It scared the shit out of me! It was the strangest thing. Nothing like that has ever happened to me before."

Michelle and I just looked at each other in amazement. Michelle turned to my husband and said, "Let me tell you a story Joe." She excitedly described to him her butterfly encounter, and I followed up by sharing mine as well. At this point it was clear to all of us that none of this had been a coincidence. It appeared that Ryan had been a very busy little spirit. This thrilled my husband! You could see it in his eyes and hear it in his voice; at long last, Joe *believed*. That night at the awards dinner, he shared his butterfly story with anyone who would listen, because when a miracle happens for you — you can't wait to share its magic.

Butterflies, like frogs, are another powerful symbol for transformation. In many cultures, butterflies are associated with the soul; they are seen as the departed spirits of our loved ones and ancestors. The emergence of the adult butterfly, symbolizes the freedom of the soul at the time of death.

The next morning I found myself thinking about Joe's miracle as I tidied our bedroom. I wandered into the little alcove where our window seat is and sat down. It was then that I saw something move out of the corner of my eye. I turned my head to the right, and noticed that a tiny yellow butterfly was perched on the frame of a poem I have titled *To My Grown Son*. Slowly, I reached my hand out toward it. When I rested my fingertips on the frame, the butterfly gracefully climbed onto my index finger.

I watched in wonder as the butterfly slowly fanned its wings. I knew that this was Ryan's way of validating the previous day's events, and the fact that I had found it perched on that poem was especially significant to me. It was then I thanked Ryan for the beautiful miracle he had used to convert Joe from a casual observer to a full blown believer.

I walked the butterfly across the room, opened the sliding glass door and stepped onto the deck. It never moved from its perch on my finger.

Softly, I whispered, "Ryan, you sure earned your wings with that one." I reminded him that his sister was the hold out; I said, "If you can get that Pollack (aka Joe) to believe — you can do anything!" With that, the little butterfly flew away.

Now that Joe had joined my "crew", I felt certain that it was only a matter of time before Katie did too. Transforming her mind set however would be no easy task; when it came to his sister, Ryan had his work cut out for him. I wasn't particularly worried about it though, after what we'd experienced so far, I felt certain that he was ready and up for the challenge.

33

IT'S ALL ABOUT KATIE

KATIE WAS A TOUGH nut to crack, but eventually Ryan found the appropriate way to reach out to her. Ryan loved his sister. This wasn't always evident to the naked eye, because like most boys, Ryan enjoyed pretending that he didn't. More often than not, he would use playful, teasing antics to express his feelings for her. But there was also a protective, gentler side to their relationship, which was the part of their bond that Katie treasured, and missed the most.

Ryan was still Ryan; the only thing that changed when he died was how we perceived him. His personality/soul/spirit remained the same, including his feelings for Katie. I knew Ryan wouldn't give up until she acknowledged his efforts to make her understand.

Ryan's earlier attempts in reaching out to her had been mischievous: He left her a feather next to a pile of dog poop one day, she found dead birds next her car — in lieu of receiving a single feather, and he gave her toads/frogs — but he left them in her window well croaking as loud as freight trains.

Ryan landed the perfect opportunity to turn his strategy around that August (2005). It was then that their stepbrother called to tell Katie that he was bringing his family to Michigan for a vacation. They live on the west coast, so they don't visit often. He wanted her to join them in Traverse City, so that everyone could spend some time together.

Katie was hesitant about going. She hadn't been to Traverse City in three years. The last time she'd seen her father had been at Ryan's funeral.

The Reason

Katie was nervous about making the trip alone, because she and her brother had always traveled and spent time with their father as a team. She was apprehensive about doing these things by herself.

I encouraged Katie to go and explained to her that her stepbrother and his family were her future. I reminded her that he was her only sibling now, and that building a good relationship with him would be important. Over the next few weeks, we spent a fair amount of time talking about his visit and even pre-planned a few fun activities she could do with her nieces. As their vacation drew closer, Katie became more comfortable with the idea of driving to Traverse City alone to spend time with them.

Joe did a thorough check of Katie's vehicle, and made sure it was ready for her trip. On the day of her departure, we made sure she had a good map, a charged cell phone and check points to call home from so we could keep tabs on her progress. I gave her a big hug and reassured her that everything would be all right. Katie hugged me back and then went on her way.

The minute she left the driveway, I was on my knees praying for her safe journey. I told Ryan, "You stick to her like glue Buddy and keep her safe. Help her, and give her signs like you give me — show her that you're there...she's scared and needs to know how close you truly are to her. I believe in you Ryan, and know that you will do your best."

I went to the cemetery to do my watering, and repeated my request to him there. On my second trip to the water spout, I found a bright yellow feather in my path. Yellow feathers symbolize cheerfulness, mental alertness, and maleness. This was a sign that my prayers had been heard.

Katie phoned me at both checkpoints, and again when she had made it safely to her destination. She sounded happy and relieved to have made the trip solo, without incident. I was confident that her visit would go equally as well.

A few days later, Katie called to tell me all about her nieces and shared with me the fun things they had been doing together. The weather was sunny and warm and she confirmed that she was having a good time. The level of excitement increased in her voice as she began to describe for me a few of the signs that Ryan had sent her way.

Katie told me that she and her stepbrother had been in the boat together when a large, white feather had floated across the water to them. The next afternoon, following a speed-boat ride, there had been a large white crane sitting in their dingy as they approached the dock. I could tell by Katie's tone that it made her feel special to know that Ryan was taking the time to send her signs. This did much in the way of reassuring her that he was there too.

The visit was short and before we knew it, Katie was on her way back home. She remembered to call us at both check points as promised. A third call was made later to inform us that she was sitting in a traffic jam. Katie told us that she was going to call her grandpa because he would probably know an alternate route she could take.

About 20 minutes later Katie called again. She told me that she hadn't been able to contact her grandpa, but on a hunch, she'd taken the Bay City exit. As soon as she left the expressway, she had felt panic set in; worried she'd made the wrong decision. It was then that she noticed the *Monarch butterfly*.

The butterfly had flown up to the front corner of her windshield, and it remained there as she drove around the entire loop of the exit ramp. Katie said that this had reassured her that she had taken the right exit. At the end of the ramp, she stopped and quickly scanned the highway signs posted there. She was relieved to find that she was at a junction for the main road she was looking for. It was then that the butterfly suddenly took flight, and headed in exactly the same direction she was about to take. Katie knew this was another sign from Ryan, helping to guide her home.

Katie arrived, safe and sound, about an hour later. We chatted for awhile and then she scurried to her room, anxious to download her pictures from the weekend. It wasn't long before we heard Katie call to us. She sounded excited, so Joe and I hustled down the stairs and went straight to her room. When she saw us, she pointed directly at her computer screen. On the monitor, was a picture of Katie holding her niece. I noticed briefly that her niece's shirt had butterflies on it, but then I quickly zeroed in on the ball of light resting on Katie's left shoulder. The image was large, and white — yet transparent. It was obvious to all of us that this was another spirit light picture, especially for Katie.

All weekend Ryan had bombarded her with the many signs she had grown to recognize and understand. These signs had been delivered with a kinder, gentler approach, portraying the protective big brother she missed so much. It was clear from the look on Katie's face that the weekend's events had officially made her *a believer*.

The light from my daughters smile filled the room and my family's hope overflowed as we took in the photograph before us. Yes, a picture can often be worth a thousand words, but in this case, one word said it all: *LOVE*.

(left) A Spirit Light photo especially for Katie, August 2005. (On Katie's left shoulder)

(below) October 2007. Ryan continues to watch over his sister... (Spirit Light on her left shoulder)

October 2008 – Ryan told me in a reading that he was
in a place with "a lot of ivy"...

Five days after my reading, Katie returned home from her
trip to Ireland — with these pictures

34

PUSHING FORWARD

THE SUMMER SOON FADED into fall, and the shifting seasons reflected the changes within us. Like trees shedding their leaves — Joe, Katie and I shed the remaining pieces of armor we'd been clinging to since Ryan's passing. Time and transformation had taught us that these shells no longer served a purpose. We realized now, it wasn't the outside world we needed protection from; it was our own thoughts and feelings that were capable of doing the most harm.

I could see changes in both Katie and Joe, and I knew that believing completely in the miracles had enabled them to push forward. This assured me that we were now all firmly on the path of recovery, and that enabled me to take my next step. I decided that autumn to address the photos the police had taken, which were tucked away at the top of my closet.

In the past year, I had thought a lot about the pictures, off and on, as I continued to wrestle with my choices. I finally realized that it was time to view the pictures and put the events of that day to rest. It was a relief to have made my decision, ending the internal debates. I felt ready to address any remaining fears and hoped that the pictures would provide closure, something I was still looking for.

Joe was still at work when I got them out of my closet. I was prepared to look at them alone, and had always known that I would; I couldn't imagine having anyone there when I did. I sat on the floor and my hands shook as I opened the packet of pictures. As I flipped through the stack, one by one, a state of numb detachment came over me. I could tell that the pictures had been edited to soften them for my review. I felt faint when I finished, and soon realized it was largely due to the fact that I had been holding my breath the entire time. It is impossible to describe how it made me feel to see my son in that way — but I can confirm that viewing the pictures did give me closure.

I remember standing up and taking a few deep breaths. Then I looked through the stack of photos a second time, because I knew I would never have the nerve to do it again. When I was done, I put them back into the envelope and then set them on the dressing table inside my bedroom closet.

I walked to the living room and sat down. About 30 minutes passed before I could even register what had happened. When reality finally hit, I collapsed into a heap on the floor. Like a wounded animal, I howled and moaned as racking sobs overtook me. The horror of my son's final moments had brought to life every raw emotion I had buried deep inside myself. I had to purge my pain or risk the threat of never being able to let it go. Maxx protectively curled up next to me, and we lay there together until my sobbing finally subsided.

Joe arrived home roughly an hour or so later. He took one look at me and knew that something was terribly wrong. I had to confess that I had been looking at the pictures the police had taken. I then asked him to build me a large bonfire, so I could burn them. Joe never skipped a beat. He walked over to me and pulled me close. When our embrace dissolved, he headed directly outside to start the bonfire.

I went back to our bedroom and got the pictures. On my way out, I stopped to grab a few of the feathers that had been given to me (by Ryan), and put them in my pocket. I met Joe outside, at the rear of our property, then watched as he walked away so I could do what I had come there for.

Maxx stood with me as I pulled out the stack of photos. One by one, I dropped them into the flames. When the pictures were gone, I reached into my pocket and tossed the feathers I had brought with me into the flames too. I did that because I wanted to cleanse the air of the pain and horror I had released into the atmosphere by burning the pictures. Doing this made me feel better, and that was all that really mattered.

I made sure that everything was thoroughly burned before Maxx and I walked back to the house where Joe was waiting for us. We spent the rest of that evening ensconced in our home as I slowly worked through the events of the day. It took me several months to shake off that experience, but eventually I was able to do so. Even now, I can honestly state I am not sorry I looked at the pictures — I'm just sorry that they had to exist at all.

I went with Katie to a S.O.S. (Survivors of Suicide) meeting the following month. She had made the choice to go, and I went with her for support. This was a huge step for Katie. During that meeting, she addressed her brother's suicide openly for the first time. She listened to other siblings and family members share their stories about how suicide had affected their lives. Hearing their stories helped her to see that she wasn't alone. This experience taught Katie the value of spending time with other survivors, because overcoming this type of death is traumatic — only those who have been through it can truly understand.

We both made huge strides in our recovery that fall. Katie continued to go to the S.O.S. meetings alone, and I took down the mailbox at the cemetery. I removed it because I felt that it had served its purpose. As painful as it was, I knew that we had to continue pushing forward. I trusted that Ryan's spirit would be there to help us over the rough spots, and prayed that my growing spiritual foundation would provide the strength needed to deal with the rest.

The Reason

The holidays were just around the corner so I braced myself for the rough waters ahead. I needn't have worried; Ryan had a very special Christmas planned for me. There were more lessons ahead and loose ends to be tied up before the New Year commenced.

35

SOMETHING OLD, SOMETHING NEW

FAMILIES GATHER TOGETHER DURING the holidays, and that is what makes them difficult for those who grieve. Assembling family members makes the absence of your loved one more noticeable. It's kind of like building a puzzle with one lost piece. Looking at the finished product, you can't ignore the fact that something is missing.

My experience has been that it doesn't matter how much time passes, you will always be somewhat conscious of the void created by your loved one's absence, regardless of place or time. It is one of the truths of death, which is important to know and accept. It will take time and experience with your loss to find a way to deal with this reality, but like everything else that's tied to grieving, you will discover the answers if you continue to work through it.

I found that lighting a candle at each holiday gathering, and mentioning that it was to honor Ryan's memory, helped me adjust to his absence during these occasions. Discovering a way to pay tribute to my son without putting a damper on the joy of the occasion benefited everyone. I think it is best to acknowledge the "pink elephant" in the room, and be done with it. It seems to relax the atmosphere and provides the opportunity to talk freely about the deceased. People take their cues from the bereaved, so don't be afraid to take the lead and tell them what you need.

There is no point in trying to sugarcoat how death affects our lives. It serves no purpose. Grief "is what it is." I once spoke to a mother whose son had been gone for over 25 years; she still got choked up talking about him. While sharing her story with me she confirmed that the holidays, as well as her son's birthday and death date, could still be difficult for her at times. She was only one of many grieving people to share those facts with me. I will be forever grateful for their honesty, because it is easier to adapt our lives to truth, than it is to lies.

There are many fallacies surrounding death and the proper way to deal with those who are mourning. One in particular is that grieving people will get upset if you mention their deceased loved one in conversation. Nothing could be further from the truth! I jumped at the chance anytime I had the opportunity to hear or see anything about Ryan. If people had something to share that was "new" to me, it was even better. I especially treasure the new pictures and videos I have been given of Ryan since his death. I consider them precious gifts, and they have provided abundant healing for this condition (grieving) that knows no cure.

One of my favorite stories regarding a gift of something "new" happened just before the Christmas holiday in 2005. Joe was on second shift at the time, and on that particular evening I had kept myself busy cleaning the house as I waited for him to get home. I went about my chores and soon found my thoughts drifting to memories of Ryan. To keep things on a positive note I concentrated on what I should ask Ryan to give me for Christmas. I made my request specific, and asked for something new about him that I had never seen or heard before. I suggested a picture, but I told Ryan that I really didn't care what form it came in.

It was late when Joe arrived home. He took off his coat and work boots before wandering into the kitchen where I was unloading the dishwasher. He laid a few things on the kitchen counter, and then went to the refrigerator to find something to eat. We spent a few minutes making idle chit-chat. When the dishes were all put away, I took on the job of sorting through the things Joe had left on the counter. As I did this, he casually mentioned that he had cleaned out his tool box at work, and it was there that he had found some pictures of Ryan. He said that because there were two copies of the same photo, he was sure that *I had never seen them before,* so he had brought them home.

I hadn't noticed the pictures until he mentioned them, because he had laid them face down in the bottom of his pile. Knowing now that they were there I quickly dug them out for scrutiny. Sure enough, there were two prints of the same picture, and they were new to me! But that wasn't all; in the photo, Ryan looked old — with deep wrinkles on his forehead. This triggered a siren to go off in my head. I was instantly aware of the fact that this was the "older" Ryan that Lori had seen in her dream — the dream where she'd held the book with the moving pictures.

Grinning from ear to ear, I reveled in the glory of my latest miracle. One picture with two distinctly different purposes: 1) my Christmas gift had been delivered, and 2) another loose puzzle piece had found its way home. I was the lucky recipient of a *miracle jackpot*! I was so thrilled; it was all I could do to keep myself from bouncing off the kitchen walls.

I couldn't wait to show Lori. Early the next morning, I called her to ask if I could drive over and show her something. She could hear the enthusiasm in my voice and without hesitation, encouraged me to come right over. I was so excited I didn't even bother to change my clothes. Fifteen minutes later, I was standing on her front porch still clad in my pajamas.

Brimming with anticipation, Lori ushered me quickly into her living room. We sat down on the couch, and it was then that I reached into my purse and pulled out the picture for Lori to see. She was amazed and elated to behold the part of her dream that had actually materialized.

We found ourselves alternately laughing and crying as we looked at and discussed the photograph together. It was truly phenomenal. When we hugged each other goodbye, I told Lori that Christmas gifts didn't get much better than that. It's a good thing I didn't put any money on that statement, because as it turned out — I was wrong.

Ryan appears "old" in the photo Joe found in his toolbox.
The wrinkled forehead and crow's feet depict
the older Ryan that Lori saw in her dream.

36

MIZPAH

ASKING FOR SOMETHING NEW about Ryan for Christmas hadn't been my only request. I still could not let go of my desire to see him, and I asked for a personal visit every chance that I got; Christmas was no exception. I had done everything imaginable to try and talk God into granting this request. I even quit smoking! My attempts at bargaining thus far had been unsuccessful, but that hadn't discouraged me from trying.

Christmas came and went. It was a good holiday due to the fact that we all did much better that year. Time was proving to be a good healer. We split our time between family and friends and I allowed their love to fill some of the emptiness I carried around inside of me. I wasn't due back to work until after the New Year, so I focused on staying busy, occasionally indulging in some of my favorite memories of Ryan. One memory in particular kept resurfacing.

It was of a day late in the summer of 2001, the year before his death. Ryan and I had spent the entire day together, just the two of us. He had played chauffer and we spent most of that morning and early afternoon shopping. When we got home, he helped me take the solar cover off the pool. We washed it, and then hung it on the fence to dry to prepare it for storage. After that, Ryan had washed his truck. It had been a great day for us and I still think about it a lot, just because it had been so wonderfully normal. No drama, just the two of us hanging out and horsing around.

Ryan must have known how special this day was to me, and the fact that I relived it often. I believe that is what prompted the next chain of events. There was a message he needed to give me and he decided that the best way to deliver it would be to recreate one of my favorite memories. So on Wednesday, December 28, 2005 — Ryan took me shopping.

The idea to go shopping started pestering me on a Monday afternoon. I called my friends Ellen, Lori and Judie, to see if I could plan a little trip for a Wednesday outing, but no one was available. I couldn't shake the thought that the lack of available companionship was how it was meant to be. Company or not, I knew for a fact that I would be going anyway, due to the persistent urge I could not, and did not ignore.

On Wednesday morning, I climbed into my car and headed north toward Saginaw. Right away, I sensed Ryan's presence. I listened to the radio as I drove, and noticed that many of the songs played came straight from my playlist. My destination was the Hobby Lobby store, but about halfway there it was "given" to me that I should do some antique shopping. I didn't really know of any antique stores in Saginaw, so I shrugged off that notion and proceeded to stick with the original plan.

Several miles from my intended exit, I noticed a billboard advertising an Antique Mall. It was located on the same road as Hobby Lobby, so I quickly altered my plans to honor my gut instincts. I smiled knowing that something besides my passion for antiquing was responsible for the sudden turn of events. I mulled on this as I parked the car. I noted also that my sense of awareness had greatly increased during the drive, and this filled me with anticipation as I made my way inside.

I wasn't in the store 10 minutes when I saw something flash out of the corner of my eye. I turned my attention toward the origin of the flash. It had come from a showcase on my left that contained a full array of jewelry. Right away, I noticed a small gold pin in the shape of a crescent moon with a single star nestled in the curve of the moon.

Set in the center of the star was a pretty, blue stone. This pin very much resembled my "Ryan ring," the one that I purchased in Puerto Vallarta. I felt sure that it was the reason I had been sent there.

Curiously, the showcase was unlocked, so I reached inside and picked the pin up. In my mind, I said to Ryan, "I guess you are taking me shopping today aren't you Cowboy?" I was touched and amazed that finding this gift had been so effortless. Needing validation, I asked for a sign that he had brought me there for this pin. I didn't have to wait long for my answer.

I walked about five steps forward and then turned a corner. Directly to my right was a little table. A white lace handkerchief covered the table top and on it laid a single, beautiful turkey feather. I looked up, down, and all around, to see if the feather had fallen off of something else; I found nothing. This feather was for me; it was my sign. I blinked wildly to hold back my tears. It overjoyed me to have received my validation with such speed!

The Antique Mall was large, with many small dealer booths. I spent the next few hours browsing each one as I looked for Ryan's little gifts. I found some real beauties, but just when I thought he could never top the pin, I laid my eyes on the *real reason* for this shopping trip.

Hanging on the wall of a small and cramped booth was a poem, yellowed with age in an 8x10 frame entitled *Mizpah:*

MIZPAH (Genesis XXX1-49)

Go Thou thy way and I go mine,
Apart, yet not afar,
Only a thin veil hangs between
The pathways where we are.

"And God keep watch 'tween thee and me"
This is my prayer;

He looks thy way, He looketh mine,
And keeps us near.

I sigh sometimes to see thy face,
But since this may not be,
I'll leave thee to the care of Him
Who cares for thee and me.

Unable to choke back my tears, I let them flow freely...*How this poem spoke to me!* I stared at it in amazement for what seemed to be a very long time, reading the poem over, and over again. The message it gave was not what I wanted to hear, but it was clearly something I needed to know and grow to accept. Ryan can only use what is available to him in the physical world, so I could only imagine his relief in finding this valuable tool — for both of us.

I am lucky to have a love as strong and pure as the one that I share with Ryan. It is this love that has allowed us to communicate in a way I never thought was possible. One of my favorite quotes states, "Where there is Great Love, there are always Miracles" (Willa Cather). I am living proof that this is true. *I believe.*

December 2005 — Ryan took me shopping, The Crescent Moon pin and Mizpah poem are the items he guided me to in the antique store.

MIZPAH

GENESIS XXI:49

Go thou thy way and I go mine,
Apart, yet not afar,
Only a thin veil hangs between
The pathways where we are.

"And God keep watch 'tween thee and me"
This is my prayer;
He looks thy way, He looketh mine.
And keeps us near.

I sigh sometimes to see thy face.
But since this may not be,
I'll leave thee to the care of Him
Who cares for thee and me.

37

I've Got Your Number

THERE IS ALWAYS A danger of slipping backward in any type of recovery. Accepting that I would not receive a spirit visit from Ryan was difficult for me. It was a huge disappointment and this threatened to put me on the slippery slope of a relapse. I had no desire to re-enter that prison of pain, so I reached for my toolbox and pulled out everything I could find to keep myself upright and steady. I was not alone. Ryan extended a helping hand and it was due to our collective efforts that I was able to hold fast and avoid the black hole.

Ryan had a plan to keep me focused, and it involved the use of *numbers* to further expand our range of communication. To initiate my awareness he started showering me with triple digit numbers of the same value (ie.111, 222, 333). I initially noticed this on digital clocks, but then I started seeing triple numbers everywhere: on license plates, sales receipts, advertisements, mailboxes, etc.

Once I was trained to notice them, they began to appear in groups of three. I would look at the clock and see that it was 2:22 PM. This might be followed by an invoice that ended in 444. The final sign might be receiving change at a cash register in the amount of $1.11. It didn't take long for me to catch on. Finding numbers in groups of three felt like a game, and playing it with Ryan reassured me that he was near.

Ryan has his own style, and I had grown accustomed to the fact that his use of repetitive signs usually meant that I hadn't looked deep enough to grasp the full lesson intended. It wasn't long before I began to question Ryan's use of numbers. I thought, "What if each number has its own special meaning, like the feathers?"

I headed to the bookstore hoping to find something there that could decipher this mystery for me. Naturally, I found what I was looking for in the Metaphysical section; it was a book titled *Angel Numbers*, written by Doreen Virtue, Ph.D., and Lynnette Brown.

This was a great discovery! The book decodes numbers from 0 thru 999. The authors explain "...that angels give us messages in the form of number sequences...you may have noticed that you frequently see the same numbers...every time you look at a clock, glance at a license plate..." Without hesitation, I purchased the book and headed for home.

It was during this lesson I learned that if Ryan used a combination of different triple numbers (555/111/333) it was just his way of saying "hello." But if I received the same exact number, three times in a row, triple digit or not, I knew to look up its meaning in my *Angel Numbers* book.

One of my favorite number stories originated in a dream on the morning of February 11, 2006. In the dream, I'd been given a list of tasks to do. I was going through the list item by item, but somehow jumped from #6 to #10 just before I woke up. Upon awakening, I clearly remembered the number 10. I could not recall the other details of the dream, but a mental image of that number preoccupied me all morning.

This happened on a Saturday, which is the day Joe and I generally go out to dinner. Throughout the day I considered several restaurants for our evening out. For some reason the Crossbow Inn kept coming to mind. It seemed like a good choice, but when Joe got home from work, he was tired. He suggested that we go to a favorite restaurant of mine that serves Chinese food. It's close to home and the service is always fast. I knew that it had been a long day for him so I just agreed.

We got into the car to go, but I really wasn't in the mood for egg rolls, so I asked if he had any other ideas. He then suggested Cranberries, which is fairly close to home, so we headed in that direction. It isn't usually that busy there, but the restaurant was packed when we arrived. We put our name on the waiting list and then sat at the bar to have a cocktail. When we finished our drinks Joe turned to me and said, "Let's go to the Crossbow." I smiled to myself thinking I should have just voiced my opinion earlier and stuck with the original plan.

We arrived at the restaurant and found that there was only going to be a short wait, so we sat at the bar and chatted while we enjoyed another drink. The Crossbow Inn is Joe's "Cheers"; everyone knows him there because he's been a regular customer for over 25 years. This fact is why it astonished me when Joe asked to see a menu; I thought he'd have it memorized by now. I handed him one from the stack that was sitting next to me. Imagine our surprise when he opened the menu to find a $10 dollar bill was inside! Of course, this prompted me to tell him about my morning and the dream I'd had. The $10 dollar bill was my second sign, so I knew I had a third one coming (Ryan continued to give me signs in three's).

Later, as we prepared to pull out of the restaurant parking lot, I nudged Joe and pointed to the radio. The CD was playing song #10! We laughed lightheartedly. I also noticed that there was a full moon, and shared with Joe that I'd recently made the observation that Ryan was especially active whenever full moons occurred. My day had certainly been filled with enough activity to prove that theory right; but Ryan wasn't finished.

Once home, we decided to watch a movie. After an hour or so, I put the movie on pause so I could get a glass of ice water. Joe used the break to make a quick trip to the bathroom. I was in the kitchen putting ice in my glass when I casually glanced over to the clock on the stove. My jaw dropped when I saw that the time was 10:10 PM. I then looked above the stove to the clock on the microwave. In that second, the time changed to

10:10 PM! I started yelling for Joe, because I needed a witness. Joe rushed into the kitchen. As if on cue, our coffee maker clock suddenly flipped to display 10:10 PM too. We stood there in amazement, surrounded by the number 10. A wave of unconditional love washed over me. The rush of emotion was so intense I could feel it permeated my soul. I spoke aloud to Ryan and said, "Thanks Buddy. I love you too."

I knew from experience that I needed to look up the number 10 in my *Angel Numbers* book, and so I did. It said, "You're receiving Divine guidance from God through thoughts, ideas, insights, or what's called *claircognizance* (knowing facts without knowing how you receive the information). Stay positive about the messages you receive."

This made sense to me because before going to bed the evening before, I'd prayed for help regarding several different things, but my primary focus had been to ask for help in finding my life's purpose. I'd said, "Please give it (the answer) to me in a dream or any sign you can. I will remain open."

This message in conjunction with the events of the day reminded me of a phrase my parents have pummeled into my brain since child-hood — "Be careful what you wish for, for you will surely get it!" I'm happy to acknowledge that in this case they were right.

PART FOUR

MOVING TOWARD ACCEPTANCE

38

SEDONA

IT IS SAD TO say that more often than not, it takes a tragedy or life altering event for us to stop and examine the course our lives are taking. "Who am I?" and "What am I doing here?" were two of the questions I began asking myself soon after Ryan's suicide. His death had stirred a desire within me to seek out my true life's purpose. Subconsciously, I had always felt that I was meant to do something more, but what that specific something was had always eluded me.

It had been almost four years since the suicide, and although I had made great progress, I was still searching for the answer to those two questions. I felt stuck and couldn't seem to get myself going in any direction outside of the status quo. I was still fighting with my weight and various health issues, all of which seemed to be magnified by a winter that wouldn't end.

What I needed was physical and mental rejuvenation, so I planned a little vacation centered on those needs. Picking my destination had been simple. One of my girlfriends had raved about a vacation she had recently taken to Sedona, Arizona. While there, she had spent a few days at a luxurious spa and highly recommended that I go there for some R&R.

Sedona is a very spiritual community, offering a wide variety of spas, salons, and retreats. Anything and everything related to the mind/body/spirit connection can easily be found there. The town itself is surrounded by the beauty of the red rocks, but the uplifting power of the Vortex meditation sites are what have made it internationally famous.

Vortexes are energy centers that assist prayer, meditation, and mind/body healing. These meditation sites are locations where energy flow exists on multiple dimensions; they are not electric or magnetic, although they are often described that way. There are Upflow, Inflow, and Combination Vortexes, and each type offers its own spiritual properties.

It was my hope that experiencing the Vortex energy would help to get me unstuck in my grief and provide the mental and physical healing I needed. As wrong as it was, I also could not help myself from praying that I would see Ryan there. With all that spiritual energy around, I figured it couldn't hurt to ask...

On March 12, 2006, I arrived at the Phoenix airport. The transportation service I had booked to drive me to the Mii Amo Spa, at the Enchantment Resort in Sedona, was there waiting for me when I disembarked. The driver also picked up three other women who were headed for the same location.

It was on the drive to Sedona, that I received my first sign. We were on the freeway, heading out of Phoenix, when I glanced to my right and noticed a lone freight car with "RYAN" painted in huge black letters on the side of it. I was feeling a little lonely so this gave me a big boost. Before leaving home, I had invited Ryan to accompany me to the 'land of Cowboys and Indians'. This sign confirmed that he had decided to join me.

We arrived at the resort, and I was taken to my room right away. It was beautiful, but I didn't have much time to enjoy it because the meditation lesson I had pre-booked was scheduled to begin within the hour. A member of the resort staff directed me to the spa, and it was there that I received my second sign. At the spa, everyone is assigned a locker to use during their stay. I was given locker #19 (Ryan's age at death). I immediately recognized this as a way for him to revalidate his presence there.

My meditation lesson went well, but I found that I was having a tough time keeping my mind off of Ryan. After meditation, I ate dinner, and then retired to my room for the evening. I was exhausted, but didn't sleep well. Despite my fatigue, I managed to get up early the next morning in time for the scheduled power walk at 7:30 AM. I had wanted to languish in bed, but something forced me up and out the door.

It was cold outside, and the only other person to show up for the power walk besides myself was a woman from Toronto named Marcia. We took to each other right away, and soon were chatting as if we'd known each other for years. I found myself talking to her about Ryan, and felt compelled to share my "butterfly story" with her. Marcia told me that her nephew had recently lost his wife, and that a story like mine would be helpful for him to hear. She and I talked a little about the hope that signs from the other side provide, and after our discussion, I felt re-energized.

Marcia and I parted ways after the power walk, and I headed back to the spa for breakfast. One of the women I had met on the drive to Sedona approached me while I was eating in the dining room. Her name was Terry. She was very warm and friendly, and she sat down to visit with me while I finished my oatmeal. During our conversation, she told me that her first husband had committed suicide. This opened the door, and we discussed both of our tragedies openly.

Because Marcia had given me such positive feedback regarding my butterfly story, I decided to share one of my miracles with Terry too. She had tears in her eyes when I finished. I apologized for making her cry, but she shook it off and explained that the tears were only because my story had touched her so deeply. Terry told me that she hadn't talked about her ex's suicide in a long time, but stated that doing so had really made her feel better. She wiped her tears and then laughed telling me, "I've been so emotional since I got here. I don't know what's gotten into me!"

After lunch, I had what is referred to as an Aura Soma reading. I was walked into a room that had several wire racks attached to the wall. These racks were filled with individual glass bottles, each containing a different colored liquid. The liquid was a mixture of plant color, essential oil and flower essences. I was asked to select four colors/bottles.

In Aura Soma, "you are the colors you chose," meaning that the colors we feel drawn to will reveal our talents, gifts and life lessons. My reading was based on the colors I selected: royal blue, red, turquoise and yellow.

The woman giving the reading was named Bhahta. I had only just sat down when she noticed, then asked about, "Ryan's ring". She wanted to know if I was aware of its meaning. I told her that I wore it in memory of my son, but had no idea that it was representative of anything outside of its personal meaning to me. Bhahta then explained that my ring was symbolic of the high priestess (tarot card).

The high priestess heightens our awareness of the intuitive side, the inner knowledge and wisdom we are born with, or seek to gain. She brings to us the knowledge that we must look inside ourselves, and not to others, for guidance. Bhahta said that the fact that I had chosen to purchase and wear this ring in honor of my son was significant, because it directly related to the bottles I had selected. Having said that, she proceeded with my reading by describing for me the meaning behind each of the colors I had chosen:

- ✓ **Royal blue:** Signifies a highly intuitive side. I was told that the knowledge gained from using my intuition would be used to write a book, enabling me to share my experiences with others.

- ✓ **Red:** Represents my struggle. Though frustrated by my limitations, I had the ability to push through my hardships and move forward.

- ✓ **Turquoise:** This color symbolizes balance and understanding — something I was very close to achieving.

✓ **Yellow:** Stands for wisdom from knowing, and removal of guilt. I would take my knowledge and use it to embrace the goodness of life. Eventually, I would see everything come full circle.

Bhahta was able to read Ryan's energy. She told me he was very happy, but sorry for all the pain that he had caused. She added that Ryan was instrumental in bringing me to my life's purpose, and that the paths of spirituality and intuition are something that he drives home to me. Now, he is *my* teacher.

In a word: WOW. This woman was a complete stranger. The only information she'd been given was that I wore a ring in memory of my son. I was completely amazed by the reading. It was amazing to have gained so much information in one sitting. It left me feeling more focused and happier than I had been in years. So far, my trip to Sedona had been worth every penny spent.

I enjoyed various beauty treatments over the next day and a half, and made the time to do some hiking in the red rocks. It was during my first hike that I received my third sign. Along the trail, I found one of my largest heart rocks ever. The rock was perfectly shaped, and was huge in comparison to the others in my collection.

I hiked for almost three hours and was exhausted when I got back to my room. I would have enjoyed a nap, but there wasn't any time. I had signed up to attend a lecture being given on the Vortex meditation sites, and I had to hurry in order to get there in time. The speaker was coming from the local university, and I was looking forward to learning more about the infamous energy sites.

The lecture was very interesting and I soon discovered that the Vortex energy was responsible for my sleeplessness and renewed obsession with Ryan. The speaker discussed the fact that the Vortexes magnify, who and what we are, and any challenge or issue we were dealing with. He said that this happens so that we can come to terms with those issues and move forward. Any emotion or feelings you bring with you are greatly exaggerated by the Vortex energy. This explained why my grief felt so huge; since my arrival, its intensity had increased tenfold. It also explained why everyone I spoke to felt so emotional. I had no doubts when it came to accepting the content of his lecture material. Most everything he said had already proven itself to be true.

The following morning I awoke early and soon found myself in familiar territory — fighting through the jungles of guilt. This thought process had become a broken record, always the same, but never resolved. I decided to make a conscious effort to break that cycle, and reached for my journal so that I could write down all the guilt-driven thoughts I possessed. It was time to get them out of my head and onto paper where I could address them. My list began with my divorce from Ryan's father, and ended with the fact that my son had died alone in his room. The whole lot went down in black and white, and when I was finished, I wrote:

> "Everything I know now doesn't do me any good because I can't use it to save you...it haunts me that I had to lose you when I see things so much clearer now. God, please help me... forgive me. Help me to be a better mother, and wife...Please help me to get it right for Katie. I can't fix what happened — so please — help me to live with it."

I read what I had written several times over, and then attempted to address the items I had listed, one at a time. Doing this forced me to recognize that most of the items I had written down did not warrant the lifelong punishment that guilt had wanted me to attach to them.

Leaving my guilt unaddressed had created an obstacle within me, and it was hindering my ability to move forward. I needed to reconcile these items in order to forgive myself, as I had forgiven Ryan.

This was a lot to take in at once. I needed to clear my head, so I got dressed and headed out for one last hike. I climbed to the top of the "Coconino woman" rock formation, and then stood in awe of the panoramic view before me. The beauty of the landscape and its peaceful silence moved me to tears. I sat down and let myself cry. It felt good to purge my pain in a place that was so healing.

The answers to my questions were being answered in Sedona. With them came the realization that Ryan's spirit was just as real as the red rock surrounding me. The only difference between the two — was in terms of physical matter. This trip had taught me that spiritual connection does not rely on matter; it is about energy and a person's state of consciousness. Faith is what pulls it all together, because that is the element which "...sees the invisible, believes the incredible, and receives the impossible." With this epiphany came tranquility, and a deep sense of devotion.

The next day I packed up and prepared for the trip home. I shared the ride back to the airport with another woman from the resort named Lisa; she was a friend of Terry's. During the drive, Lisa told me about her brother who had taken his life eight years ago. She said that at the time of his death she had directed her attention to the needs of her parents and her own growing family. This left her very little time to grieve herself. Telling me her story proved to be therapeutic for Lisa, and when we parted at the airport, she hugged me and thanked me for listening.

Our discussion reinforced the importance of talk therapy and the fact that people need people. I firmly believe that the stories of other grieving individuals are our best resources for comfort and knowledge. Listening to the experiences of others promotes insight and provides emotional support. We learn from each other, and the benefits gained from sharing, greatly enhance the odds of a successful recovery.

On the plane ride home I sat next to a man who had lost his only daughter and grandson in a car accident. I knew it was no coincidence that we were put together for the 4-hour flight. Like the others, he just needed someone to share his story with. At the end of our discussion, the purpose for this trip became crystal clear to me. It had given me the opportunity to share my miracles/lessons/stories with others, and this had enabled me to recognize their ability to transform sorrow into hope, not just for me, but also for most anyone who was grieving.

This knowledge provided the perfect ending to a trip that will always be thought of as a time of self-discovery and spiritual growth for me. I got everything I went to Sedona for, except a visit from Ryan. Somehow, it didn't matter, because like the red rocks — *I know he is there.*

39

MIND OVER MATTER

I RETURNED FROM SEDONA feeling like the "energizer bunny", and that is no exaggeration. I directed most of my newfound energy into the gym, and began working out with a personal trainer. When I combined this fitness regimen with the healthier diet I had adapted at the spa — I started getting results. Two months later I was 15 pounds lighter, off all medications (except for the antidepressant), and successfully controlling my back pain with nothing more than ibuprofen. I felt like a new woman, and the changes that were taking place weren't limited to my physical appearance.

My intuition and awareness levels were off the charts. I walked around feeling as if every cell in my body had become hard wired to the universe; I noticed everything. I had also noted that my dreams were much more vivid, in terms of both color and detail. I attributed all of these remarkable changes to the Vortex energy I had experienced in Sedona. Jokingly, I told my girlfriends that if I could figure out how to bottle that stuff I'd be rich!

Soon after my return from Arizona, my sister Steph invited us to her house for dinner. She had also invited my parents who had just returned from Charleston, South Carolina. After dinner and dishes, we all congregated in the kitchen/living room area. I sat down at the kitchen table, directly across from my sister. I fiddled with a napkin on the table in front of me while listening to the various conversations taking place around me. After a few minutes, I looked up to ask Steph a question, but stopped abruptly when something behind her caught my eye and captured my attention.

Over Steph's left shoulder, in the center of her kitchen, I recognized Ryan's grey "Polo" sweatshirt and blue jeans. I immediately knew the sweatshirt, because it was the one item of his, I'd taken to Sedona with me. My brain said, "Oh, Ryan is here," and then I realized — *Oh my God, RYAN IS HERE!* I could see his outline due to the clothing he wore, but everything about him was transparent. I could not make out his face, but I knew that it was him. The whole thing was so quick! In less than five seconds he was there, then gone.

To say that I was rendered speechless would be a gross understatement. All those months and years of asking and praying for a visit, and then, out of nowhere, *when I least expected it* — Ryan pops in to say hello...FABULOUS! I must have been sitting there with my mouth open, because Steph asked me what was wrong. I looked back at her and said, "I just saw Ryan in your kitchen!" It was absolutely one of the most phenomenal and memorable moments of my life.

I was riding high after Ryan's visit. I looked forward to sharing it with Elaine at my next reading. I had an appointment for a Mother's Day reading, and that was just around the corner. I now limited my readings to twice a year: Mother's Day and my birthday. These dates are six months apart and create a good balance. As my healing had progressed, I was careful to exercise the rule of moderation.

As enthralled as I was with the new world Ryan had exposed me to, I had to remain mindful of the fact that I still lived in this world. The key to understanding and working with contact from the other side is to remain focused on that fact. Our life is here, and we must direct our time and attention to fulfilling our own life's purpose. Their loving communication provides the opportunity to heal as we transition ourselves away from the loss of their physical presence, to the spiritual connection they can provide to ease our pain and suffering.

As always, I prepped Ryan for my visit with Elaine as the day of my reading drew closer. I recited the date and time of our appointment to him both at the cemetery and in his room while speaking into the mirror. I leave nothing to chance when it comes to spending time with Ryan.

Elaine greeted me at the door with a warm, welcoming smile. I had brought two of my heart rocks to share with her. She told me that holding them gave her goose bumps, and then added, "That's how you know it (spirit contact) is real." When "show and tell" was over, we sat down to begin the reading.

The first thing Ryan showed Elaine was the color blue. Blue didn't really mean much at that moment, except that his eyes are blue, and I always think of them. I wrote it down for later, remembering that things don't always make sense at the time of the reading. Next, he brought up the color yellow. I had been thinking of painting his room yellow, so that fit.

The next item given was the name "Burrows." It sounded familiar to me, but I didn't know why. Then Elaine asked if I knew a William, Billy, or possibly Bill? Before I could answer, she started laughing and said, "Never mind — He keeps screaming Billy, Billy, Billy — I guess I'd better get it right!" Ryan followed this with "pink princess," which are two words I immediately associated with Katie, so I wrote this down along with the last few items hoping she could shed some light on their meaning for me later.

Elaine looked at me quizzically and said, "Grapefruit juice?" I told her that the night before I had thought about drinking a glass of grapefruit juice, but hadn't because it had been too close to bedtime. This was an odd reference, but I just assumed it was Ryan's way of letting me know he had been watching me the night before, because I had reached into the refrigerator to get the juice, before deciding against it.

Ryan said that Katie had a new book, a book he wanted her to read. He told Elaine that someone else in the family would read it, but to Katie it would be new. I explained to her that I had bought a new book on sibling grief for Katie not too long ago, and had read it myself before giving it to her. Just recently, I had put it back in her room, although she had not read it yet. I was certain this book was the one Ryan was referring to.

A large volume of information was exchanged during this reading, but as always, Ryan was saving the best for last. Just before our hour was up, Elaine asked me "Do you have a big green plant in your house somewhere?" I told her yes, I had only one big green plant, it was silk, and that I kept it in the master bedroom. She said, "Ryan wants you to put it in the corner." I looked at her in amazement. I was so caught off guard by her statement I could scarcely breathe.

For the past week and a half, I had looked at that very plant — at least two or three times — *and thought to myself,* "I should put that in the corner of Ryan's room, by the floor lamp." I had never said it out loud — *only thought it.* I tried to explain this to Elaine, and when I did, she simply repeated his request, "Well, he wants you to move it there — you should put that plant in his room."

She didn't get it, but I did. It wasn't about the plant, or moving it to his room. The message here was about telepathy...*Ryan could read my mind.* This was the circumstance behind many of the messages given to me during the reading: the color yellow for his bedroom, wanting the grapefruit juice, moving the plant...all pertained to thoughts I'd had, not things I'd said or done. This was a huge revelation! I took the time to more carefully explain all of this to Elaine. When I finished, she just looked at me smiling and said "Happy Mother's Day."

Katie was home when I got there, and I read her some of the things that I had written down, but hadn't been able to place. She knew almost every item! Katie was thrilled to have received so many messages from her brother. She clarified these few things for me:

1. The "pink princess" was actually a toy TV that she and a girlfriend had seen in a store while out shopping the week before. They had joked about it because it was soooo Katie!

2. "Burrows" is the name of the main character in one of her favorite TV shows "Prison Break." She had just watched it the night before.

3. Billy — was Billy's Roadhouse. One of Katie's friends had recently gotten a job there; she and her friends had been hanging out at "Billy's" the past few weekends.

This reading re-affirmed for Katie how closely, and lovingly, her brother continues to watch over her. I took this opportunity to explain to her that she would never have to worry about him missing her college graduation, wedding, or any important life event. I told her, "Ryan wants you to know he is there, everyday, and always will be."

I learn something valuable every time I reach out to Ryan; one of the things I learned this time was his capacity for patience. Telepathy had been the very first thing he had tried to communicate to me — over four years ago — and it had taken me this long to completely grasp the totality of his message. The old Ryan would never have taken that amount of time for anything, but the new Ryan had proven to me, time and time again, how devoted he was to our recovery.

I was so proud of my son; I felt the need to do something that would prove to him that his efforts to help us had not been in vain. A few months later, I got the opportunity to do just that, and all I had to do to accomplish this was BELIEVE.

40

B ELIEVE

In Sedona, I had been told that I would write a book, but at the time, I was being pulled in another direction. For many years, I had directed my creative efforts into interior design. When Ryan and Katie were little, I had been a stay-at-home Mom and had spent much of that time remodeling and decorating my first two homes, then successfully flipped them for profit. After my divorce, I worked in the furniture industry which also called upon my decorating talents. All of the time and effort I had devoted to these endeavors had me convinced that my purpose was tied to these creative skills.

Just before Ryan's death, I had started a small business specializing in home staging and budget decorating services. Everything came to a complete halt after the suicide, but when I returned from Sedona, I decided it was time to start the business up again. My expectation was that getting this business off the ground would somehow validate my return to the human race. I felt that in doing so, I could prove to Ryan that his efforts to help me hadn't been in vain.

I found myself struggling and lacked the motivation to get things going. It felt more like a chore than an exciting adventure. I found myself continually questioning my decision. Was it fear holding me back, or was I going down the wrong road altogether? I finally resolved that it didn't matter if it was the wrong choice — I was keeping my day job. If the business took off, I'd do it full time, if not, I would at least eliminate the weight that restarting it had put on my mind.

The Reason

I shared my career frustrations with my friend Jann one day, and she suggested that I participate in the Women's Expo event scheduled for September (2006) to re-launch my business. I mulled it over and decided that committing to this event would force me to get things up and running. My heart wasn't in it, so I asked for a sign to help convince me that this was the right thing to do.

The local newspaper was sponsoring the event, so that is where I went to sign up. Unfortunately, when I got there, no one seemed to know what to do. Finally, the security guard called upstairs to have a marketing person come down to assist me. I sat down and thumbed through a magazine as I waited for help to arrive, all the while thinking, that as far as signs went; things weren't looking too good.

That thought no sooner passed through my mind, when I had the sudden urge to look up. When I did, a woman I recognized met my gaze. She and I had been in the same Tai Chi class together. Her name was Shelia, and I had completely forgotten that she worked at the newspaper.

Sheila walked over and embraced me in greeting. I was so glad to see her! She inquired as to what brought me there, and I told her I was trying to sign up for the Women's Expo, but that no one really seemed to know what to do. She took me under her wing and things started to fly into place! After we had taken care of business, I smiled at her and stated, "You won't believe this, but you were my sign." I shared my little story with her, and because she already knew a little about my son, she looked up and said "Thanks Ryan!" It was great, and it made me feel secure in the fact that I had done the right thing by signing up for the Expo.

I had no idea of what I'd gotten myself into, but luckily my friend Melanie had agreed to share the Expo booth with me, and our combined efforts made the job a little easier. I had no props or signage, so I spent all my free time orchestrating and constructing the proper items to accurately display the aspects of my business. The weekend before the Expo,

I pushed hard to complete my design boards. This kept me up late, so I turned on the television for company. I channel surfed and ended up watching the movie "Serendipity". John Corbett, Kate Beckinsale, and John Cusack played the main characters in the movie. It had a great story, and watching it kept me entertained and sufficiently alert so that I was able to finish my project.

The next morning, I awoke with a very strong urge to drive to Lexington. It's a little town on the east side of the state and about a 90 minute drive from home. Judie and Barrie had spoken of Lexington often; it was one of their favorite places to visit. They enjoyed the beach there and the beauty of Lake Huron. I had been thinking about them a lot lately, because in June they had sold their home and moved to Albuquerque, New Mexico. My loneliness for them and my need to take a break from the Expo preparations made going to Lexington seem like a great idea.

Katie was home for the holiday weekend, and she agreed that a little day trip would do us both good. We printed a map off the internet and were soon on our way. We took our time, and even stopped at a few garage sales along the way. It wasn't long before we reached our destination. It was getting close to lunch, so I parked the car and we browsed the town looking for someplace to eat.

We walked down a side street and discovered a little restaurant named "Serendipity," but it was closed. I laughed when I saw the name, and shared with Katie how I had watched a movie with the same name the night before. We walked back to the main street and decided to get a snack at a coffee shop a little further down the street. I walked up to the counter to place our order and noticed that next to the register was a stack of hand bills, advertising upcoming events for the local theater. I picked one up and started to read through the list. I almost dropped my coffee when I saw that the third band listed was the John Corbett Band. His picture was on it, so I knew it was the same actor from the movie!

The Reason

I know by now that everything happens for a reason. The movie, the restaurant and now the hand bill with the actor on it. I didn't know what it all meant, but the fact that I had gotten the sign's in 3's meant something. Serendipity is synonymous with destiny, fate, and karma, so I considered that this was simply Ryan's way of validating that my decision to participate in the Expo had been a good choice, and left it at that.

Katie and I enjoyed our afternoon shopping and exploring the town. On our way home, we stopped at a little gift shop out in the middle of nowhere. It was there that I found a small 6 inch knick knack; the word "believe" carved out of wood. Its styling was more country and not the type of thing I usually buy, but something about it spoke to me. I purchased it and set it on the shelf in my office next to Ryan's picture.

The Women's Expo was soon upon me. The day before the big event, I found a gift and card in my chair at the office; they were from my friend Kathy. The gift was a figurine of a woman with the phrase "Believe when it's beyond reason to believe" embossed on the bottom perimeter of the figurines dress. I picked it up and when I flipped it over the word "Believe" was on the underside as well.

There was that word again. I felt now that I was onto another message from Ryan. Within moments of receiving Kathy's gift, my telephone rang. It was my friend Bev. She was calling to tell me that she had found something interesting in her car while cleaning it over the weekend. Bev went on to say she'd cleaned and vacuumed her car many times in the four years that she'd owned it, and that she rarely vacuums the backseat area because no one ever sits there. But for some reason she'd vacuumed the back this weekend, and when she'd lifted the floor mat, a small silver pin was lying there. On the pin, in lower case letters was the word "believe." Bev said, "Sal, the minute I saw it — I knew it was for you!"

Ryan loves to send messages through Bev, but she'd been a little tougher to train than Lori. She is very cautious and this makes her slow to react when he gives her things. Ryan's tactic with Bev is to pester her non-stop until she moves into action. Knowing her cautious nature makes her messages more valuable to me. Because when she does deliver one, I know without question that he has something of importance that needs to be communicated.

Bev told me that he had played "Devil Went Down to Georgia" and "Somewhere Out There" (songs Bev associates with Ryan) as a way to get her to call me. She had wanted to deliver the pin to me in person at the Expo, but Ryan's constant pestering had forced her to change her plan. Bev said that *clearly*, Ryan wanted me to know about it NOW.

If I hadn't been laughing so hard at Bev's story, I would have been crying tears of joy. I let her know that her pin was my third sign, and that Ryan's message was clear: Believe. This wasn't just about the Expo — it was about everything. Believe in God, believe in miracles, and *believe in yourself*. If I truly wanted to make Ryan proud and prove to him that none of his efforts had been in vain, then I had to plant my feet firmly in faith and *stay there*.

It was then that I told myself "I am going to kick some ass at that Expo" because not doing my best would be an insult, and I was *not* going to let either of us down. Our booth at the Women's Expo did very well, and I was grateful to have not only completed my quest to re-launch my business, but to also learn a very valuable lesson in faith. My days of jumping back and forth between believing and being afraid to believe were ending, and it felt great to find solid ground at last.

Ryan once came to me in a dream and asked, "Momma...Am I an angel?" I looked at my beautiful son and told him, "Yes, *you're my angel*," then planted a kiss on his cherubic face just before he faded away. Angels are messengers from God, and I'm grateful beyond words to have him as mine. To the roots of my soul — *I believe.*

41

A FEW WORDS ON FAITH

WHEN RYAN DIED, I was a "green horn" in terms of spiritual development. It wasn't due to a lack of effort. My mother tried to educate me in these matters; from a very early age, I was encouraged to go to church.

My family went to the Baptist church in town. Every Sunday morning my mother would haul me there for worship. When I was about 16, I challenged a youth group leader on the topic of hell. The long and short of it, is that I didn't believe in hell and he did. Our debate brought many of my feelings regarding religion to the surface, and shortly after that discussion, I felt myself detach from the beliefs of the Baptist church, although I continued to attend services to pacify my mother.

Since then I have formulated my own idea of God and the role he plays in my life. I believe in a God of love, not in a God of judgment and condemnation. I perceive both hell and heaven as states of consciousness, not as locations; therefore, hell doesn't exist unless I create it for myself, and heaven is well within my reach at any given moment. Every action I take in my lifetime counts, and I alone am responsible for my overall life experience. God is with me every step of the way, and I need only to look within myself to find and receive his abundant love and guidance.

There is much more to it than that. But, I'm not going to tell you "*how it is*" because it is different for everybody! I believe, without reservation, that it doesn't matter what faith people belong to, because in the end, they all lead to love. I took the spiritual path of New Thought, and found a quote that sums up this choice for me: "Religion is for people who are afraid of going to hell; Spirituality is for those who have been there." (Ross V., Member of AA).

I feel that Ryan's death caused God to make purpose out of tragedy, because it was losing my son that put me on a path to enlightenment. I would follow my child anywhere, and Ryan had led me in this direction. Barrie, Judie and I discussed this at length, as they too believed this is what happened to them. Barrie described it best in an e-mail he once sent to me. He said:

"...their (Angie and Ryan) leaving so early made us look deeper than we ever did before. What am I, what is life, and why did this happen? The answer of course is that we needed to return to the Spirit that created us. How else would we have looked so deeply and earnestly? Now we are at last on the path..."

I feel it is important to provide this information about myself, because I don't know how anyone can believe in miracles without having some type of faith. For me, the two go hand in hand. My struggle wasn't about believing in the miracles and the messages they provided; it was about defending my sanity *because* I believed in them.

Please take my advice — if you are privileged enough to be the recipient of a miracle, just embrace it and don't worry about how anyone else interprets *your* experience. Plant your feet firmly in faith, and embrace the hope that God has so generously provided to you. Confucius said, "Those who are meant to understand will hear — Those who are not meant to understand will not hear". If someone is meant to comprehend the miracles as you do, they will share in your hope and happiness.

My sister-in-law comforted me one day when I showed up on her doorstep in tears. I had just left my parents home where someone had cruelly tossed aside one of the spirit light pictures I had chosen to share.

This action had crushed me, because it took my hope and twisted it into something that seemed foolish and sinister. She listened to my story and then told me that I should never "cast my pearls in front swine" (Matthew 7:6), which means you shouldn't share things that are precious to you with people who'll never appreciate them. Her words brought me comfort, and I vowed that day to never again let anyone attempt to steal or destroy my hope. I have learned to keep those who support me close, and merely accept that others may not share my point of view.

The Women's Expo was a turning point for me, one that confirmed my beliefs and verified my sanity. Now, when doubt wanders in, I refer to the words of Madeleine L'Engle to keep myself grounded, "If it can be verified, we don't need faith...faith is for that which lies on the other side of reason. Faith is what makes life bearable, with all its tragedies and ambiguities and sudden, startling joys."

42

MIRROR, MIRROR ON THE WALL

DREAM VISITS FROM OUR departed loved ones are coveted treasures. Ryan's visits are all precious to me, but one of my personal favorites is one I named after him, titled *Big Boy Cowboy*. I favor it because it combines all of my favorite elements: (1) Ryan and the ability to touch him and smell him, (2) validation within the dream content, and (3) answers to a loose puzzle piece.

It had been awhile since his last dream visit, and I had spent some time thinking about what I wanted to do when he dropped in again. Usually, I am so excited to see him I can barely think or speak, so I vowed to be prepared for the next one. I was cleaning Ryan's room one day and found myself speaking into the mirror to him as I sat dusting the items on the dressing table. I told him, "The next time you visit, the first thing I'm going to do, is look into your eyes and tell you that I love you." I know he can always feel it, but I wanted to be able to say it and then give him a big smooch. A few nights later, he gave me the opportunity to do exactly that, with a bonus gift included.

In the dream, I was standing on a fireplace ledge looking into a big mirror hanging over the mantle. While gazing into the mirror, a little pair of brown cowboy boots walked into the lower right hand corner of the mirror's reflection. I turned away from the mirror to look behind me for the source of the cowboy boots, and discovered with joy that my "Big Boy Cowboy" had joined me!

Ryan appeared as a little boy (about three years old), and he was wearing his favorite western styled pajamas. The pajama top had a brown vest, red bandana, sheriff's badge, and holster all printed right on the fabric. The pants were a bright royal blue. Ryan had topped his outfit off with the red felt cowboy hat he always wore, and he stood there looking at me — grinning ear to ear.

This time, I was ready...I took my time as I walked up to him. I placed a hand on each side of his face, looked into his baby blue eyes and said, "Ryan, I love you." I gently placed a kiss upon his lips and then looked back into his eyes with satisfaction, knowing I had fulfilled my wish to perfection. It made me so happy that I just started planting wet kisses all over his face saying "I love you" over, and over again. My Cowboy smelled and tasted like heaven, I gobbled him up and enjoyed each and every second of it.

I pulled him close to me and said, "I'm afraid to blink or let you go, because I know that you will disappear on me!" But he stayed for quite some time...I think he must have enjoyed all that smooching, because he let me do it again and again! He never spoke a word to me, but he didn't have to. To be able to hold him, kiss him and smell his sweet skin was plenty for me.

When I woke up, I ran to the photo albums, hoping to find a picture of him in those pajamas so I could share my dream with Joe. I had to go through several albums, but I finally found the picture I'd been searching for. I looked in amazement at the photo in my hands. I hadn't thought of those western pajamas in over 15 years, but I was very impressed that Ryan had, and it thrilled me that he'd worn them to validate his presence for me.

I was laughing and crying as I told Joe about my visit. I explained to him that even in my dream state, I was aware of the fact that I had successfully executed the plan I had rehearsed in Ryan's room earlier that week. It was during my story that I remembered a very important detail in the dream I had been overlooking. The mirror — I became aware of his presence because I had seen the cowboy boots *in the mirror.* This provided an answer to a very old, but very valuable puzzle piece. Now I knew that speaking into the mirror had significance.

I had never understood the innate reflex that had caused me to do that in the first place, but after Ryan's visit, I decided to look into it further. I put "mirror gazing" into the internet search box and discovered some very interesting information. I was especially intrigued to discover that Dr. Raymond Moody, author of *Life after Life,* had done extensive research in this area.

Throughout history, people have attempted to communicate with the dead using mirrors as a type of medium. The ancient Greeks (Homer) wrote about a ritual process that they used involving an area described as a "necromanteum," which contained a cauldron-type container. This container was filled with water or oil which provided a reflective surface into which the individuals would gaze to contact their deceased loved ones.

Dr. Moody studied the details of this process and created what he calls a "psychomanteum." His replication involves a mirror, comfortable chair, and a darkened room. In this process, the participant cannot see their reflection directly in the mirror, because it is hung outside of their direct line of vision — but they do look into the mirror to experience spirit contact. Participants will sit in the psychomanteum from 45 minutes to an hour. There are no guarantees of a visitation when using this method, but many participants feel it helped them in one way or another.

There is much more to the psychomanteum process than I have outlined here, but this provides the basic idea behind it, and where it originated. For me, it was a loose puzzle piece that had at long last been given an explanation. I had started speaking into Ryan's mirror simply because I had always felt connected to him when I did. It intrigued me to discover that unknowingly, I had been utilizing a historical process in doing so.

I am always fascinated when I stumble across this type of information, because I find it interesting and educational. It just proved to me that for centuries the desire to make contact with deceased loved ones has been a natural response to death. That makes me *normal*, and in a world that wants to make me feel otherwise, I found this fact downright comforting. It's all about perspective, and so far, an open mind had been one of my greatest assets. I don't expect everyone will see things the way I do. I try not to judge, and encourage others to do the same. Opinions are like...Well — *everybody has one.*

"Big Boy Cowboy" — Ryan visits me in a dream,
wearing his favorite pajamas

43

JRW4EVR

THE BOND BETWEEN RYAN and I remained strong. Haphazardly, we established our own form of communication by utilizing the different signs he had given me over the years: numbers, feathers, heart rocks, frogs, herons, and butterflies. Once these basics were established, I learned to look deeper into each sign and was able to attach a more concise meaning to several by using the resources available (i.e. internet, books). Sometimes, depending on the history of a sign, Ryan and I would attach our own meaning, for sentimental purposes.

Along the way, I defined something I refer to as a "moron sign." These types of signs speak for themselves. I love them because they actually spell the message out for you — leaving no room for doubt. Remember, the only thing spirits have to work with is what is here in our physical world. So, depending on the message, it can be difficult for them to make their point. Because of this, I am especially thankful for personalized license plates, and the following story is a good example of why they are one of my favorite forms of communication...

We were just about at the end of our fifth year of grieving when I got a phone call from Katie at work. She had called to tell me that she had forgiven Ryan. This was a huge step forward for her and I was proud that Katie had been able to work through such a difficult issue. I could tell by the sound of her voice that it felt good to have finally removed this enormous weight from her shoulders.

After my conversation with Katie, I sought out my friend Kathy. I found her working diligently in her cube, and quickly shared the good news with her about Katie. When I was done talking, Kathy asked me, "Do you think Ryan will leave now that Katie has forgiven him?"

I knew the answer to this question, because I had advanced to the point where I understood that spirits don't "go" anywhere. Their energy is always with us. I calmly explained this to Kathy, but couldn't seem to shake the rising anxiety her comment had initiated. We finished our conversation and I headed back to my desk. Because it was the end of the work day, I prepared to leave for home — her comment nagging at me the entire time.

I let myself think about it once I was safe inside my car. I knew better than to let an innocent comment get to me like that! I tried to brush it off; a lot had happened and I just needed to relax and let it go….but I found that I couldn't. During the drive home, I had to keep telling myself to settle down. About two miles from my exit, I couldn't stand it anymore, so I blurted out loud, "Ryan, please don't leave me, at least not now, I don't think I'm ready."

No sooner had those words left my mouth when a blue Equinox pulled in front of me on the freeway. I could not help but notice the license plate, and when I read it, I almost fainted. It was a personalized plate: JRW4EVR. Deciphered, those are my son's initials (Jeffrey Ryan Wecker) with the promise of forever (4EVR). No mistaking that one — it was the best "moron sign" ever! What better way to say, "*I'll always be here Momma.*" Tears formed in my eyes as a whoop of happiness escaped from my mouth. Who would believe this one?

I wanted a picture so bad I could taste it, but I had a slight problem. I was driving on the expressway going about 70 mph and the Equinox ahead of me was doing the same. This forced me to take a mental picture, but I vowed that if I was fortunate enough to see that license plate again, I was going to get some kind of proof that it existed. I had reached my exit, so I veered off and watched as the other vehicle continued east-bound, slowly disappearing from sight.

Six weeks later, I got my second chance. I had returned home from the gym, and was headed for the house — when the urge to jump on my bicycle came over me. It was a beautiful day, but I'd already had a good workout and didn't really see the need for more exercise. With each step, these thoughts accelerated from an urge to a mental push toward the bike. I stopped in my tracks and let intuition take over. It was then that I realized I was going for a bike ride — whether I wanted to or not.

I jumped on my bike and peddled toward my parents' house, which is just a mile down the road. My dad and nephew were outside and waved as I rode by. Seconds later, I was at the street corner and right there in front of me, making the same turn, was that blue Equinox! I pedaled that bike like Dorothy trying to outrun the tornado in the *Wonderful Wizard of Oz*. Faster and faster I went, so as not to lose sight of the vehicle. Luckily, for me, it pulled into a driveway about a half mile up the road.

A woman had exited the truck, and was walking to the mailbox at the end of the driveway. I peddled up to her, smiled and climbed off my bike. "Sorry to bother you," I said, "But would you mind telling me the story behind your license plate?" She smiled back and told me that it represented her late husbands' initials. She'd had the license plate made in his memory; he'd recently passed away from a complication follow-ing knee surgery.

We talked for a few moments and then I shared my story of how I'd seen her on the expressway several weeks before. I explained that her license plate had been my sign. She told me that she understood this, because she had received a few signs herself since her husband had passed. We shared a few stories of spirit contact and it reminded me of how common these types of experiences were turning out to be. All in all, it was a pleasant conversation. I thanked her for her time, intending to go back later with my camera to get a picture of the license plate for my story. Truth is, once home, I became caught up in my day, and forgot to go back.

Days turned into weeks, and before I knew it, a whole year had passed and I still did not have my picture. In August of 2008, I made it my mission to catch her at home and get that picture taken. Almost two weeks passed, and then one day I noticed a white vehicle in her driveway with the same license plate on it. Evidently, she had purchased a new car and I was still looking for the old one! I went up to her front door and knocked.

When she answered the door, I asked if she remembered me. I reminded her that I was the crazy woman on the bike last summer that'd stopped to ask about her license plate. She remembered me and we had a little laugh. I asked her if it would be alright to take a picture of the license plate. I explained that I had written a story about it and would like the picture for "proof". She understood, and led me around to the front of her garage, which was open.

We walked inside the garage, and there on the window sill was the old license plate from the Equinox. She'd had another one made for the new vehicle. She handed the old plate to me. "Here," she said, "you can have this one." I was thrilled! This was so much better than a picture! I looked at the renewal sticker in the lower corner of the plate. It was orange and the month JUL was stamped on it. July — that was the month of Ryan's birth date. Could this get any more perfect?

I keep that license plate in a safe place, but take it out from time to time just to remind myself that miracles really do happen. When you can hold proof in your hands like that, it's hard to argue otherwise.

My "moron sign" — Ryan found a way to reassure me
that he would always be near...

44

WRAPPING IT UP

WHAT DOES ALL OF this really mean? Well, my message — although different — is really quite simple. I believe our deceased loved ones want to help us with our grief as much as we want and need to be helped. Notice the word *help*, because that's all it can ever be. Spirits can't heal us, but we can heal ourselves knowing that what we thought was lost to us forever is still here, somewhere in the air that we breathe. Allowing the experience of spirit contact to become a part of your recovery can boost your ability to move forward; this makes it a healing *tool*.

If something is broken, you can't fix it without the proper tools, so I provided a complete toolbox in Chapter 16. It is filled with helpful things to give anyone struggling with grief a head start on their recovery. Spirit contact is different. It isn't for everyone. Utilizing this unconventional method of help is only possible if a person is open and willing to recognize the miracles that surround us each and every day.

My stories provide specific examples of how spirit contact takes place. This should make it easier to recognize if similar things are happening to you or someone you know. Many grieving people have shared their stories with me, and I found that butterflies, music, feathers, rainbows, and numbers, are common tactics employed to get our attention. It is worth repeating that the spirits are always in control of when and how these signs are delivered. That is to remind us that they are *special gifts*; if we could order them on demand they would lose their significance. The more you receive, the more you will come to realize, that the timing is what makes the miracle.

Spirit contact is not only possible, it does in fact happen to many, many people — I'm just not afraid to talk about it. I have documented close to a hundred incidents, but took special care to select those that I felt best told our story and were able to provide some type of evidence, or witnesses, to validate that these events did in fact take place. I feel it is my purpose to share these stories, and in doing so I have taken on the burden of proof. I believe that Ryan provided me with the physical items that he did (heart rocks, spirit pictures etc.) to help validate these experiences, not only for me — but for those I was meant to share them with.

Skepticism can be a good thing. It makes us cautious and forces us to look deeper when we are in unfamiliar territory. In the beginning, we were very skeptical. We wrestled with ourselves plenty when it came to believing in the signs and miracles we received; but with time and experience, we learned to embrace their healing power and quit trying to figure it all out. Not everything is meant to be explained, sometimes we just have to accept what is and take our own message from it.

It is important to point out that not all spirits are as active as Ryan is. I believe the level of activity I received was directly tied to my life's purpose...I was told in Sedona that the knowledge gained from using my intuition would be used to write a book, enabling me to share my experiences with others. The signs, miracles and lessons Ryan has conveyed to me are those experiences, and I am glad I listened to my intuitive side or I might have missed it all. I was destined to write this book, and my inspiration comes from wanting to help others see and utilize the many tools available during the grief process. I want to reassure people that if spirit contact does happen, they are NOT crazy — just loved.

Believing in the afterlife has nothing to do with one's ability to accept death; it's about understanding death's transformation — from physical form to the pure energy of spirit. The difficult part of any life change lies in our capacity to adjust from one set of circumstances to the next. Spirit contact can help bridge the gaps during this life change, making the transition less painful, and providing the hope to rebuild.

The bulk of our recovery had to do with the ability to transform our thought process. In order to leave the past behind and deal with the pain, we had to be open to new ideas, and willing to take the action required to change our lives. There can be happiness and joy after death, but people must make the choice to pursue it. Understand that destiny is not out of one's control; it is simply a case of taking the reins. In the words of Henry Ford, "Whether you think you can or think you can't, either way you are right."

Support throughout the grief process is necessary and I encourage you to take all the help you can get — *wherever* it may come from. Take advantage of support groups and any counseling services available. Reach out to your friends and family, they want to help, so let them. Our ability to ask for help plays one of the most important roles in recovery. When you ask in prayer, remember:

- ✓ You must ask with heartfelt sincerity.

- ✓ You must "believe to receive" (Matthew 21:22). This means you have to know in your heart, with complete certainty that your prayers are heard and will be answered.

- ✓ Be patient — assistance will come when the timing is right.

- ✓ You may not get what you want, but you will always get what you need.

- ✓ Prayer is the conduit of miracles.

The Reason

When tragedy occurs, people have a choice. They can work through the pain or they can succumb to it. I won't lie — it is much harder to work at grief than it is to let it engulf you. That's why they call it WORK. Take it from a survivor: Work through it now, and address the pain, or it will follow you forever. Don't try to make sense of your loss, simply accept what you cannot change and trust that *with time and effort,* you will find a way to recreate your life. Recovering from loss doesn't mean you're forgetting your loved one, it just means you're learning to remember them without all the pain.

In the beginning, our love for each other was all we had. I didn't know that it is going to be the only thing we'd need. When I look back, I realize that learning this was the most valuable lesson of all. When you understand that love is the most important tool you've ever been given, you will never need anything else, in this world or the next. Love was the key which opened the door out of my misery into hope.

Ryan is my teacher, my angel, and my reason for taking a journey that began with the loaded question, *"Where did my son go and is he alright?"* I can now say with confidence that, "Only a thin veil hangs between the pathways where we are...," and he appears to be doing quite well. Somewhere inside of me, I have always felt this to be true. It simply takes awhile for the brain to grasp — *what the heart already knows.*

My Beloved Son — J. Ryan Wecker
7/9/82 – 6/28/02

Epilogue

There are so many ways to describe Ryan; I hardly know where to begin. He was my first child and only son. When he was little, he loved playing with his Lego's, Matchbox cars, Transformers, and Tonka trucks. Ryan also liked John Deere tractors, country music, model cars, cheeseburgers and chocolate shakes. "JR" and "Big Boy Cowboy" were a few of his nicknames.

As an adolescent, Ryan watched a lot of movies and ate plenty of Taco Bell. He laughed at Monty Python, Garfield, Beavis and Butt-Head, and The Simpsons. His interests included architecture, shipwrecks, and the Civil War. He loved building models and had all the latest electronic gizmo's and games like Nintendo and Game Boy.

When Ryan received his driver's license, he chose a Ford pickup truck for his first vehicle, and got mad at me when I told him he couldn't hang the confederate flag in the back window. He worked out at the gym and played golf in his free time. He always had a part-time job and managed to spend every penny of the money he earned.

Ryan was smart. He was in the gifted program in elementary school, and in the honors classes in high school. He graduated with honors and completed his first year of college at the University of Michigan-Flint before he died.

My son grew into a loving, intelligent, handsome, funny, hard working, and personable young man. Ryan never had trouble making friends, but he always seemed to be most comfortable around adults. I always thought of him as an old soul in a boy's body. I believe he always struggled with this; the old soul wanted to do the right thing, but the boy in him always pushed the limits as he looked for approval from his peers.

Like any other teenager in high school, Ryan wanted to be popular and hang with the "in crowd". The problem was that the "in crowd" in this case was nothing but trouble. They promoted the use of alcohol, steroids and a drug called GHB. The last 3 years of his life were a struggle due to the peer pressure this created and Ryan's internal need to strive for perfection. He tried to escape the pressure by self-medicating. I fought hard to maintain control of the situation, but before I knew it, our problems had escalated to a point of no return.

When it came to the drug GHB, I had no idea what I was dealing with. It was so new that the doctors didn't even know what it was. We had to rely on the internet to obtain our information. It is a form of the drug ecstasy, which mimics the effects of alcohol. It couldn't be detected in a blood or urine test, which is why the kids used it.

I found myself battling with other parents, school officials and law enforcement in efforts to open their eyes to the drug problem that existed in our high school. It didn't matter what I did, or who I talked to, *no one* would listen or help me. I was fighting for my son, but it felt like a losing battle — which soon became a nightmare I couldn't escape.

I put Ryan in rehab twice during his senior year. He saw a counselor and I tried to monitor his friendships and whereabouts 24/7. I lived each day consumed in fear. It terrified me to have Ryan out of my sight. I tried everything that I was aware of at the time to get the situation under control, and I fought to help him get his life back on track. I have no regrets for the actions I took to help him; my only regret is that it wasn't enough.

His substance abuse created problems in both the medical and legal systems. We tried a variety of doctors and hired lawyers to try to help him work through the problems his addictions had created. Sadly, both of these systems terminate parent's rights as soon as a child reaches 18 years of age. The older he got, the more we found our hands were tied. Luckily, Ryan was receptive to our help and followed our advice, or we would have been completely helpless to provide the assistance he needed.

The fact is that as much as we would have liked to think that we were in control of Ryan's life, the truth was that we were not. In the end, Ryan made his own choices, and we had to learn to live with them. It all came down to his free will, and that is something no one, not even God, can control. Understanding the power of free will has helped me to accept the suicide. When guilt tries to take me under, I focus on the fact that Ryan made the decision to end his life, while the rest of us fought to save it.

I miss everything about Ryan: his beautiful blue eyes, how the scent of his cologne lingered in the rooms where he walked, seeing his name written on cards and notes, calling him on the phone, sharing our private jokes, rubbing his stiff gelled up hair, playfully biting his ears, hearing his voice call out to me when he walked in the door, his brilliant smile, the special way he always made me feel...HIM.

The advice I have to pass along is — love your children. *Never let them leave without kissing them goodbye and telling them that you love them.* A woman I worked with a few years before Ryan died gave me this guidance. She had lost her son several years before in a car accident. I took her words to heart, and on the morning of the suicide, I heard them in my head when I was turning the door knob to leave the house. These words stopped me in my tracks and I turned around, descended the stairs, and kissed both of my children goodbye before leaving for work that day.

This action saved my sanity. I didn't see Ryan's face that morning because his bedroom was dark, but I kissed him and when I turned to leave his room — he called me back for another hug. I went back and sat on the edge of his bed, playfully biting his ear before hugging him again. My last words to Ryan were, "I love you Buddy. Don't worry, everything will be alright — don't I always make things right for you?"

He didn't give me the chance to do that for him, but he didn't leave me empty handed either. He gave me that memory, and a chance to say goodbye. A part of me will always long for my son, and crave his contact. Rumi said, "There is a path from me to you that I am constantly looking for." In my case, Ryan dropped the breadcrumbs and I followed them...

There is so much more to Ryan than that moment in which he took his life; I couldn't let the act of suicide be the only thing that would be remembered about him. My son was a generous and loving person in life, and in the afterlife, all those qualities remain. This book is a testament to the love, faith, and hope he poured into our lives, fueling our recovery and moving us forward. This is his legacy, to us, and to every soul that our story touches.

Ryan–
Love You Long Time (L.Y.L.T.),
Momma Mia

Bibliography

Kemp, Penny. *The Epic of Toad and Heron*. Toronto, Ontario, Canada: Playwrights, Canada Press, 1972, Foreword.

Virtue, Doreen, and Lynnette Brown. *Angel Numbers*. Carlsbad, CA: Hay House, 2005, pp.16, back cover text.

The Compassionate Friends National Organization, "Worldwide Candle Lighting." (Online). Available http://www.compassionatefriends.org/News_Events/Worldwide_Candle_Lighting.aspx

Survivors of Suicide, Hampton Roads Support Group, "Legend of the Crane." (Online). Available http://www.sos-walk.org/sos/crane.htm

About the Author

Sally Grablick lives in Southeast Michigan; this is her first book. Her entrepreneurial spirit has taken her down several different paths professionally — but personally, she is steadfast in her mission to help others navigate their way through loss. To further this cause, a percentage of the earnings from *The Reason* will be donated to reputable grief support and suicide prevention organizations.

For more information on grief recovery/support, the author, and her book — visit http://www.thereason-book.com.

Sally can be contacted at sallygrablick@gmail.com.

CPSIA information can be obtained
at www.ICGtesting.com
Printed in the USA
FFOW02n0336080416
23072FF